"I truly marvel at Lori's ability to
Word. Yet again, the Lord has gifte
A Word for Your Day. Each devotion c
ture through the Bible and sit closer to my Lord."

—*Dawndy Mercer Plank, WIS TV anchor*

"Lori excavates gems from all 66 books of the Bible—not only discovering them but fashioning them to sparkle with the light of truth and the beauty of worship."

—*Stephen Davey, pastor-teacher, The Shepherd's Church*

"Lori Hatcher has matched insights gained from many years of daily Bible study with a unique package: biblical truth and encouragement gleaned from each book of the Bible. She provides the context for each book, combining encouragement with challenge."

—*Leslie Stobbe, writing coach, editor,*
and author of God Moments in My Publishing Life

"Lori Hatcher has done it again! Her relatable writing style and real-world examples bring life to each word she has chosen to illustrate the essence of each book of the Bible. It will inspire and encourage you to explore every book in God's Word with joy and expectation."

—*Jeanne Devine, director of women's ministries, Cornerstone Fellowship*

"Bold truth in a blanket of love."

—*Lisa Baker, author of* Someplace to Be Somebody

a word for your day

66 DEVOTIONS TO REFRESH YOUR MIND

LORI HATCHER

Our Daily Bread
Publishing.

A Word for Your Day: 66 Devotions to Refresh Your Mind
© 2024 by Lori Hatcher

Interior design by Hillspring Books, Inc.

Library of Congress Cataloging-in-Publication Data
Names: Hatcher, Lori, author.
Title: A word for your day : 66 devotions to refresh your mind / Lori Hatcher.
Description: Grand Rapids, MI : Our Daily Bread Publishing, [2024] |
   Summary: "Women's ministry speaker Lori Hatcher returns with 66 easily
   digestible devotions weaving masterful storytelling with the beautiful
   truths of Scripture. In only 5 minutes a day, you'll take a brief look
   into each book of the Bible and be reminded of a spiritually relevant
   word to ponder for that particular book."--Provided by publisher.
Identifiers: LCCN 2023011210 | ISBN,978-1-916718-12-8
Subjects: LCSH: Bible--Devotional use. | Bible--Meditations. | Devotional
   exercises.
Classification: LCC BS617.8 .H38 2024 | DDC 242/.2--dc23/eng/20230710
LC record available at https://lccn.loc.gov/2023011210

Printed in Europe
24 25 26 27 28 29 30 31 / 8 7 6 5 4 3 2 1

*To Dad, who bought me a new Little Golden Book at the grocery store every
week and read each one to me until I could quote them from memory.*

*To Mom, who threw open the doors of Rogers Free Library
by signing me up for my first library card.*

*To my daughters, Kristen and Mary Leigh, who allowed me
to read aloud to them, under the guise of homeschooling,
all the great books I missed the first time around.*

*To my grandchildren, Lauren, Caroline, Andrew, and Collin, who allow me
to read to them all the great books I missed the second time around.*

*To my husband, who graciously supports my book-loving habit
with patience and grace.*

I love you all.

Contents

beginning

In the beginning God created the heavens and the earth.

Genesis 1:1

Who doesn't love a new beginning? Especially the beginning of a new year. With the orbit of the earth and the turn of the calendar page, we bid the old farewell and greet the new with a welcoming kiss. Only a second separates the previous year from the following, yet there it is—a fresh start. A do-over. A reboot.

Three hundred sixty-five days stretch promisingly before us, shining in their unmarred splendor. We breathe in their scent, crisp and clean, and we feel hope. A new year invites us to archive the difficulties of the previous year and turn our faces toward the dawn of new beginnings.

Like children on the first day of summer vacation, we look ahead to days fertile with promise, and our imaginations soar. Will this be the year our prodigal turns to the Lord? Or the year a long-awaited dream comes true? Will the prayer of a decade come to fruition? Will God reveal himself in ways we can only imagine?

At the dawn of time, the Bible tells us, God was there. "In the beginning God created the heavens and the earth" (Genesis 1:1). Hebrews 1:10 fleshes out the details: "In the beginning, Lord, you laid the foundations of the earth, and the heavens are the work of your hands."

I wonder if God's heart beat hard as He peered out over the vast expanse of nothingness, knowing that very soon, something spectacular would take its place. A sparkling world filled with promise only He could create. As we face new beginnings, do our hearts beat with similar anticipation?

Sometimes mine does. Other times, a niggle of fear gnaws at the edges of my excitement. If the previous year has been hard, I wonder if more heartache will follow. If the year overflowed with joy and blessings, I wonder if the tide will turn, pummeling my life with storms.

Whether you greet a new start with anticipation or trepidation, it's comforting to know that God has been present in every beginning. The early verses of John 1 affirm this truth. "In the beginning was the Word, and the Word was with God, and the Word was God. He was with God in the beginning" (vv. 1–2).

Revelation 22:13 tells us that *Beginning* is one of His names: "I am the Alpha and the Omega, the First and the Last, the Beginning and the End."

Whether your new year holds tragedy or triumph, you can rest in confidence that God is there. Not just in the beginning, but all the way through. Unlike the deists—who believe God set the world in motion, then stepped back to watch it play itself out—we know God goes behind us and before us, hemming us in with His presence and protection (Psalm 139:5). Nothing comes into our lives that isn't filtered through His hands of love.

We can be confident God will accompany us every step of the way—through our new year, our new venture, our new **beginning**.

i

God said to Moses, "*I AM WHO I AM*. This is what you are
to say to the Israelites: '*I AM* has sent me to you.'"

Exodus 3:14

Moses had an *I* problem.

So do we.

But not the type of *I* problem you might suspect. He wasn't a nar-cissist or characterized by pridefulness or excess self-confidence. On the contrary, as Moses wrote, under the inspiration of God, "Moses was a very humble man, more humble than anyone else on the face of the earth" (Numbers 12:3).

Can you imagine God prompting you to write this about yourself? If you were the humblest man on earth (and Moses was—God said so), you certainly wouldn't want to be the one to write about it. It would chafe against every humble bone in your body.

Yet despite his humility (or perhaps because of it), Moses got into trouble—the same kind of trouble that threatens many of us today.

Humility can be a cover for disobedience. Or a tendency to doubt God's ability to work through us. Or a desire to be asked more than once to do something.

Picture the scene: Moses fled Egypt and turned his back on his life in Pharaoh's palace. He'd tried—once—to come to the aid of his brothers, the Israelites, with disastrous results. A dead Egyptian and a bounty on his head sent him hightailing it out to the desert. There he found a job, married, and settled into a humble lifestyle of keeping sheep.

Until God showed up.

"So now, go. I am sending you to Pharaoh to bring my people the Israelites out of Egypt," God declared from the burning bush (Exodus 3:10).

"But Moses said to God, 'Who am I that I should go to Pharaoh and bring the Israelites out of Egypt?'" (v. 11).

This is where we catch the first glimpse of Moses's *I* problem. Like when the ophthalmologist clicks that little lens in front of your eyes, and everything goes blurry. Moses's humility clouded his vision.

I can't go to Pharaoh, he thought. *I'm a nobody. Why would Pharaoh, the most powerful man on earth, listen to me?*

Then God clicked on the lens Moses needed to correct his *I* problem. He answered Moses's *I*'s with a few *I*'s of His own.

"And God said, '*I* will be with you. And this will be the sign to you that it is *I* who have sent you: When you have brought the people out of Egypt, you will worship God on this mountain'" (v. 12; emphasis added). My presence, God said, is all you need to confront Pharaoh and lead the Israelites.

Yet Moses continued to declare his inadequacy.

"Suppose I go to the Israelites and say to them, 'The God of your fathers has sent me to you,' and they ask me, 'What is his name?' Then what shall I tell them?" (v. 13).

Thankfully, God held the prescription for Moses's shortsightedness: "God said to Moses, 'I AM WHO I AM. This is what you are to say to the Israelites: "I AM has sent me to you."'" (v. 14).

In this declaration, God identified himself as the name above all names *and* the power behind everything He calls us to do: *Yahweh*, the self-existent one. His first name, Elohim, hearkens back to the first chapter of Genesis, where God created the heavens and the earth. His second name, Yahweh, declares Him as "the existing one."

Often, like Moses, we struggle with an *I* problem. God calls us to do something—teach a Bible study, mentor a troubled teen, share our faith with a coworker—and we can't see past our inadequacies. *Who am I to speak for God? I've never been to seminary. I can barely parent my own kids. And I certainly haven't memorized enough verses to share my faith.*

I, I, I.

I can't do it in my own power. *I'm* just not enough.

And we're absolutely right. We can't do it in our own power. We aren't enough.

But God is.

The great I AM, the self-existing one, the almighty God who stitched the universe in place and breathed life into dust to make a man, *is* enough. And He lives within us, lending His strength and power to our feeble efforts.

He will equip us. He will go ahead of us into every opportunity He brings our way. He will accomplish His will in the world around us—not despite our inadequacies, but because of them.

"Who gave human beings their mouths?" He asked Moses. "Who makes them deaf or mute? Who gives them sight or makes them blind? Is it not I, the LORD? Now go; I will help you speak and will teach you what to say" (4:11–12).

When was the last time you said no to a God-sized opportunity because you felt inadequate? Were your eyes focused on your *I*'s or on Elohim, the great I AM?

Perhaps it's time you had an *I* exam. Maybe it's time to ask God to remove the *I*'s that cloud your vision so you can see your calling more clearly through God's *I*'s.

thanksgiving

If you ask people to name their least favorite book of the Bible, I suspect more than a few would mention the book of Leviticus. "Many a commitment to read the Bible through," my pastor would say, "was wrecked on the shores of Leviticus."

I get this. Leviticus contains page after page of instructions about ritual sacrifices, dietary laws, and guidelines for how an unholy people can approach a holy God. We discover how to determine if a skin spot is benign or leprous, how to get rid of mildew in a house, and which foods are clean and unclean.

And we read a lot about blood. Blood for a sin offering. Blood for a peace offering. Blood for a trespass offering. And what to do with the fatty lobe of the liver, the crop of a pigeon, and a bull's entrails. Ew.

Because Christ became the final sacrifice for sin, and we are no longer under the law, is it any wonder we flip past Leviticus to get to something a little less gory and a little more relevant?

But tucked into the pages of this oft-neglected book are principles and practices worth considering.

Take the practice of offering a "sacrifice of thanksgiving to the LORD" (Leviticus 22:29 NKJV). We think about thanksgiving when we gather on the holiday, but, other than that, how often do we sacrificially recognize God's goodness to us?

Leviticus gives us the characteristics of a thanksgiving offering, which are relevant as we approach God in gratitude today. First, a thanksgiving offering is voluntary. "Offer it of your own free will," Moses instructed (v. 29). Thanks should bubble up out of a willing heart. God shouldn't have to squeeze, guilt, or coerce it out of us.

Unfortunately, most of us aren't naturally grateful. Grumbling is our default setting. But we can learn to recognize and name our blessings. Listing daily gifts in a gratitude journal or encouraging family members to share three things they're grateful for over dinner can help make us more aware of God's goodness.

Second, a thanksgiving offering acknowledges the good as well as the bad in our lives. When God gave instructions for celebrating the Passover, He told the Israelites to sweep their homes clean of anything containing leaven. Another name for yeast, leaven is what makes dough rise. In the Bible, leaven symbolizes everything bad in the world.

Yet in Leviticus 7:12–13, Moses instructs the people to offer a leavened loaf alongside their unleavened cakes. They were to raise the two loaves, the "good" and the "bad," to the Lord in thanksgiving.

If you're like me, when I list God's blessings, I write down items like health, protection, and provision. Biblical thanksgiving also includes thanking God for the parts of our lives that don't look like gifts.

By practicing this discipline, I've learned to thank God for unemployment because it taught me to trust Him as my provider. I've come to appreciate trials because they compel me to seek Him in prayer. I've come to value sickness because it teaches me to empathize with those who chronically suffer.

Third, a thanksgiving offering is sacrificial. God instructed the people to give their best animals and finest oil and flour. When was the last time you donated a significant and sacrificial amount of money, time, or effort to God's work out of pure gratitude?

We can donate money to feed hungry children because we're thankful our children have never lacked food. We can write checks to ministries that smuggle Bibles into closed countries because we're grateful for the Scripture we enjoy every day. We can volunteer at crisis pregnancy centers because we're grateful for the children in our lives.

Finally, a thanksgiving offering reminds us of the greatest gift of all, the one that should top our gratitude list every day of our lives—the gift of Jesus. Leviticus 7:14 (NKJV) says, "And from it he shall offer one cake from each offering as a heave offering to the LORD. It shall belong to the priest who sprinkles the blood of the peace offering."

Did you catch that? "It shall belong to the priest who sprinkles *the blood of the peace offering.*" Onto the fine flour that symbolizes the good gifts in our lives and the leavened bread which symbolizes the bad parts of our lives, the priest sprinkles the blood of a lamb or a goat.

The blood of the offering symbolizes Jesus, the final sacrifice, who made it possible for us to have peace with God our Father. Without the blood, we'd have no basis for gratitude. Nor would we have a relationship with God. No thanksgiving offering is complete without a heartfelt and humble acknowledgment of Jesus, the greatest gift of all.

I don't know if you underappreciate the book of Leviticus. If you do, maybe this devotion has changed your perspective. Perhaps it even motivates you to offer a thanksgiving offering to God. When you do, be sure to thank God for every book of the Bible, because even the book of Leviticus is cause for **thanksgiving**.

offerings

Then the leaders of Israel, the heads of families who were the tribal
leaders in charge of those who were counted, made offerings.

Numbers 7:2

I encountered a new concept when I began attending church with a
high school friend. There I heard the mysterious word *tithe*. As I listened to the pastor explain how God calls believers to give a portion
of their income as an offering to God's work, I was flabbergasted.

Give away a tenth of your income? In the church I'd grown up
in, most people tossed a random twenty (or five) in the plate as it
passed. But ten percent? As in, one tenth of everything someone
earned? My fifteen-year-old brain did the math on what that figure
would amount to for the average working adult. Wow.

The first chance I got, I quizzed my friend, who had a part-time
job and a regular paycheck. "Do you tithe?" The word felt awkward
and lispy on my tongue.

"Yes," he said. "Since I was a little kid."

"Why?"

"Well," he thought a moment. "Because God tells us to. Everything I have comes from Him anyway, so it's not unreasonable that He asks us to give a portion of it back to provide for the needs of the church."

His explanation made sense—for another day. "I'd like to tithe—someday—when I have more money."

"Why wait?"

I laughed. "I don't even have a job. All I get is an allowance. Six dollars a week. A tenth would be sixty cents." I laughed again. "What good would sixty cents do for God?"

"You'd be surprised." He launched into a story about a little boy who gave his tiny lunch to Jesus and how Jesus worked a miracle with it. Then my friend said, "Sometimes we have to obey even when what He asks us to do doesn't seem to make sense."

Maybe if I'd studied Numbers 7 when I was fifteen, I'd have understood the importance of giving. This very repetitive chapter describes the offerings the twelve tribal leaders brought to furnish the temple and provide sacrifices for its dedication. Here's an excerpt:

> The one who brought his offering on the first day was Nahshon son of Amminadab of the tribe of Judah.
>
> His offering was one silver plate weighing a hundred and thirty shekels and one silver sprinkling bowl weighing seventy shekels, both according to the sanctuary shekel, each filled with the finest flour mixed with olive oil as a grain offering; one gold dish weighing ten shekels, filled with incense; one young bull, one ram and one male lamb a year old for a burnt offering; one male goat for a sin offering; and two oxen, five rams, five male goats and five male lambs a year old

to be sacrificed as a fellowship offering. This was the offering of Nahshon son of Amminadab. (vv. 12–17)

By the second item on the list, I was ready to skip to the end.

If we hang in through the rest of the chapter, we'll encounter this same paragraph *eleven more times*. Numbers 7 contains eighty-nine verses—1,981 words—and almost all the verses are repeated word for word, except for one difference.

The name changes as each tribal leader presents his offerings for the tabernacle.

Why didn't Moses just list the offerings once, name the twelve leaders as a group, and be done with it?

Maybe he listed each man's name and the details of each offering because he wanted to spotlight the fact that God sees every giver and every gift. God doesn't just say, "Oh, the church congregation gave a good offering today." Instead, He sees Pat and Jennie, who gave three hundred dollars to missions this month despite having to put a new transmission in their fourteen-year-old car. And He sees Sarah, the single mother who's learning to give by faith and slipped twenty-three dollars into the offering plate. And He sees Paul, who's been tithing since he got his first job in high school. He's sending two kids through college on his blue-collar salary, but he gives faithfully every week.

Remember what Jesus said outside the temple as He taught His disciples about giving? He didn't speak in generalities. He commended "one poor widow" (Mark 12:42–44 NKJV).

When I was fifteen (and sometimes even now), I compared my giving with others' and wondered if God noticed its smallness. Do you? Maybe the amount you place in the offering plate seems insignificant in light of what others give. Perhaps you attend a church of thousands, and you doubt your offering matters at all.

Think again.

God used eighty-nine verses of the Old Testament to list individual names and what they gave to the Lord because it matters to Him.

Nothing escapes His watchful gaze. Nothing pleases the heart of the Father more than watching His children obey His commands, including bringing their offerings to His house. He sees every dollar we give, every hour we serve, and every loving act we extend.

So the next time you wonder if giving to God's work is important, remember how He allotted eighty-nine verses in the book of Numbers to list twelve people—by name—and their 342 **offerings**.

remember

Remember how the LORD your God led you all the way
in the wilderness these forty years.

Deuteronomy 8:2

As I settled Mrs. Evie in my dental chair and clipped a napkin around her neck, she glanced at me and smiled.

"My daughter brought home a new puppy. His name is Bear."

"How fun," I said. "I love puppies. What breed is Bear?"

We talked a bit about the challenges of housebreaking and puppy training, and then I got busy cleaning her teeth. When I raised the chair for her to rinse, she swished, spit, and spoke again.

"My daughter brought home a new puppy. His name is Bear."

Mrs. Evie is eighty-two years old and suffering from dementia. Many of our conversations run in circles. Every time I care for her, I notice she forgets more of the everyday details of her life.

I thought of Mrs. Evie when I read the book of Deuteronomy. Fourteen times the Lord, through His servant Moses, called His people to do what she struggles to do: remember.

Unlike Mrs. Evie, the Israelites were young, and their minds were strong. The older generation, those who had refused to enter the promised land, had perished. A new generation stood in their place.

Now the nation paused, camped at the border of the land God had sworn to give their forefathers, while God prepared them for the challenge ahead. Like a general on the eve of the big battle, Moses reviewed everything God had taught them and repeated the instructions He'd given their ancestors.

Then Moses called them to remember.

"Remember how the LORD your God led you all the way in the wilderness these forty years" (Deuteronomy 8:2). Don't forget how God has shepherded and directed your life.

"Remember that you were slaves in Egypt and that the LORD your God brought you out of there with a mighty hand and an outstretched arm" (5:15). Call to mind how He delivered you from bondage and oppression to sin.

"Remember well what the LORD your God did to Pharaoh and to all Egypt" (7:18). Think about how He has acted on your behalf, rescued you from circumstances beyond your control and positioned you to inherit an eternity free from sickness, sorrow, and pain.

"Remember the LORD your God, for it is he who gives you the ability to produce wealth" (8:18). Acknowledge that your health and strength, your ability to provide for yourself, and all the material blessings you possess come from God.

God knows we, like the Israelites, are a forgetful people. Despite His history of faithful care, we fly into a panic at the first sign of trouble. Although we've seen Him rescue, provide, protect, and preserve, when the tiniest whisper of uncertainty reaches our ears, we climb aboard the fear train and ride it down the what-if track.

We allow spiritual amnesia to wipe our memories clean of the ways God has met our needs, healed our bodies, and restored our souls. We forsake the joy and peace He makes available to us if we will only trust. We smear God's name by responding in fearful and faithless ways when danger threatens.

Because I don't want to smear His name or forget His abundant goodness to me, I put disciplines in place to help me remember.

I keep a journal, capturing for myself and my family the ways God has met my needs, guided my steps, and spoken to my heart. After walking with God for more than thirty years, I now have a shelf of journals that provide indisputable evidence of God's daily care for me.

I begin and end each day with gratitude. In prayer, sometimes aloud and sometimes silently, I thank God for specific blessings and kindnesses.

I ask God to show me the "good and perfect gifts" He sprinkles on my day (James 1:17). My life is filled with good things, but many of them slip right by me like a whiff of fresh-baked bread outside a bakery. If I stop to savor each gift and recognize it for what it is, I'm more likely to remember it later.

As often as I can, I tell others about God's care for me. Speaking these blessings aloud roots them more firmly in my memory and brings glory to God's name. Sharing them with others allows them to praise God for His mighty works. This helps them become more aware of God's actions on their behalf and helps them grow in faith and trust too. Sometimes, like my sweet friend, Evie, I forget. Practicing the disciplines of thankfulness and praise helps restore my memory.

• • •

Father, thank you for loving me. Help me never forget how you've walked beside me all the days of my life, how you've preserved, protected, and provided for me. Open my eyes to your goodness. Help me always to **remember**.

promises

Not one word of all the good promises that the LORD had
made to the house of Israel had failed; all came to pass.

Joshua 21:45 ESV

"Most of the time, I love my job."

Pam leaned across the table to snag another tortilla chip. She
dunked it in the almost-too-spicy salsa, popped it in her mouth, and
chewed contemplatively. Then she shook her head.

"But on days like today, I get so frustrated. I want to help people
plan for their future, but they have to trust me.

"Take today for example. I met with a sweet Christian man.
When we reviewed his portfolio, I saw that if he doesn't start saving
and investing for the future, he's going to be in big trouble."

"What did he say when you pointed that out?" I asked.

Pam shook her head again, dunked another chip, and chomped
down. "He said, 'God said He'd supply all my needs according to
His riches in glory. So I don't have to worry about the future. God

will take care of me. I'm claiming this promise by faith. Every promise in the book is mine, right?'"

Pam's client probably grew up singing the words to the old hymn, "Every Promise in the Book Is Mine," and he believes it. But is this song based on Scripture? Can we claim every promise as our own?

The Bible overflows with promises, probably because God loves to make promises and intends to keep every single one of them. Today's verse is proof of this. Listen to Joshua's words to the children of Israel:

"Not one word of all the good promises that the LORD had made to the house of Israel had failed; all came to pass" (Joshua 21:45 ESV).

All came to pass. Sounds like a good hook for Pam's client to hang his faith hat on, doesn't it?

Except it isn't.

Careful study reveals the Bible contains four kinds of promises: personal, universal, conditional, and unconditional. Each one is rooted in God's unchanging commitment to keep His word and accomplish His will in the world.

Personal promises are specific and directed to a particular individual or group of people. God's promise to Abraham to make of him a great nation was a personal promise. I can't wield Genesis 12 like a promissory note and demand God give me a family and land like He swore to give Abraham. His promise to Solomon to give him wisdom, riches, and an enduring kingdom was unique to Solomon himself. To expect the same from God for myself is presumptuous.

Universal promises are for everyone. Isaiah 40:8 is one example: "The grass withers and the flowers fall, but the word of our God endures forever." No matter what happens, God's word will remain.

Conditional promises require us to take action before God will fulfill His promise. Romans 10:9 is a conditional promise: "If you declare with your mouth, 'Jesus is Lord,' and believe in your heart that God raised him from the dead, you will be saved." For God to save us, we must confess Jesus and believe in His resurrection.

Unconditional promises require no action on our part. Acts 1:11 fits this description. "'Men of Galilee,' they said, 'why do you stand here looking into the sky? This same Jesus, who has been taken from you into heaven, will come back in the same way you have seen him go into heaven.'"

As Joshua prepared to lead the Israelites into the land God had promised to give them, God reminded him of His unconditional promises. "Be strong and courageous, because you will lead these people to inherit the land *I swore to their ancestors to give them*" (Joshua 1:6; emphasis added). Believe my promises, God said. Trust my word.

Sadly, some waver in their faith because they appropriate promises that aren't intended for them or confuse principles with promises. Many a heartbroken parent has feared God has failed them because they've claimed Proverbs 22:6 (NKJV) as a promise: "Train up a child in the way he should go, and when he is old he will not depart from it."

As much as we wish that God promised if we raise our children in the faith, they will embrace it, an accurate understanding of the book of Proverbs and other wisdom literature reveals God gave the books as a guideline for living, not as a guarantee of results.

Others, like Pam's client, take promises out of context and use them as a shield against the consequences of irresponsible or foolish behavior. While God has promised to meet our needs, He also expects us to save, spend wisely, and responsibly manage our finances.

God has filled His Word with thousands of promises. If we read them in context and ask, "Is this personal or universal, conditional or unconditional?" we can determine which ones God meant for us and cling to them like anchors.

Like Joshua, we can receive them as gifts, draw courage from their words, and trust God to fulfill His good and perfect will through them.

We can rest secure, knowing God always keeps His **promises**.

grieved

Now the Israelites grieved for the tribe of Benjamin,
their fellow Israelites. "Today one tribe is cut off from Israel."

Judges 21:6

Deep creases furrowed Andrea's forehead. Her usual bright smile was gone.

"Thanks for meeting me here on such short notice," she said as she plopped her purse onto the chair beside her. "I just got off the phone with my mom. Tony's being released."

Arrested for armed robbery ten years ago, Andrea's baby brother, Tony, had been in jail as long as I'd known her. We talked often about him, but usually Andrea smiled as we talked. She beamed when she told me he'd started attending Bible study and reading his Bible regularly. Her face lit up when she announced that he'd repented of his sins and asked Christ to be his Savior.

Since then, she'd often shared how he was living out his newfound faith in prison. How he and his cellmates were reading through the book of Genesis and talking about what they read. Tears of joy trickled down her face as she showed me a letter he'd sent to her and her brother, asking forgiveness for bringing shame to their family. She'd clutched the letter and said, "I think he's truly sorry for what he's done. He's not the same Tony that went into prison."

This is why I couldn't understand why she wasn't dancing around the room. "Andrea, you've been counting down the days until his release for years. Shouldn't you be smiling?"

"I would be," she said, "if it wasn't for my brother Jim. He said after what Tony did, he doesn't deserve to be welcomed back into the family. He broke Mom's heart. No amount of jail time can atone for that. But Tony's our brother, and he asked us to forgive him. I can't imagine not welcoming him home."

My heart ached for her. For Tony. For all the family. Breaks in a family relationship for any reason cause a deep sense of sadness and profound grief. It's been this way since Adam and Eve. It hadn't gotten better by the time Jacob and his twelve sons grew into a large nation.

With God's enabling, Jacob's descendants, the Israelites, had conquered the land of Canaan and settled into their respective land inheritance. But prosperity and success caused them to fall away from the Lord, and "everyone did what was right in his own eyes" (Judges 17:6 NKJV).

For one of the tribes, the Benjamites, "right" meant committing a horrific sin, one their brothers took legitimate offense at. (You can read about it in Judges 17–20, but be warned—it's awful.) The remaining eleven tribes enforced swift and terrible punishment, purging the sin from the land and shielding the rest of the nation from God's judgment. In the process, they destroyed almost the entire tribe of Benjamin. Only six hundred men survived.

Adding to the devastation the deaths and sinful acts had caused, the great rift cut off a whole tribe from the rest of the family and brought deep sorrow.

"The people grieved for Benjamin, because the Lord had made a gap in the tribes of Israel" (21:15).

Andrea grieved like this for her brother. Although he'd committed a crime that deserved punishment, once justice had been served, Andrea knew it was time to try to restore the family relationship.

"Tony's going to have to win back our trust," she said. "He has to prove he's changed, but we need to give him a chance."

The Israelites felt the same way. They gave the tribe of Benjamin another chance. They took the first step at reconciliation. "Then the whole assembly sent an offer of peace to the Benjamites at the rock of Rimmon. So the Benjamites returned at that time" (vv. 13–14).

Every family story is different, and not every family break can or should be mended. But many can.

On the day Tony was released from prison, with Andrea's gentle encouragement, Jim stood beside Andrea and their mother to welcome Tony home. He'd taken the first and hardest step of reconciliation.

Is your family wounded by a damaged relationship? Perhaps the Lord is calling you to initiate restoration. With prudence and prayer, seek God's will and His direction. Ask Him to move in your family members' hearts to bring about healing and peace. Then, through the power of God, may your family no longer be **grieved**.

refuge

"May the LORD repay you for what you have done.
May you be richly rewarded by the LORD, the God of Israel,
under whose wings you have come to take refuge."

Ruth 2:12

My spaniel-setter mix rescue dog, Winston, was learning to walk on a leash. He'd grown past the stage of biting it, trying to wriggle out of the collar, or straining like a sled dog with a thousand-pound load. Every day he grew more confident and willing to respond to my guidance.

One day I took him onto a busier street than we'd ever walked to help him become familiar with the sounds and motion of traffic.

Our walk started off well. Winston watched the cars with curiosity as he stepped out, curly ears flopping and feathery tail waving like a flag in a parade. His wet nose twitched, enjoying the new smells. He eyed a squirrel high in a tree but, wonder of wonders, didn't charge after it.

Then, in the distance, I saw trouble. Four motorcycles sped toward me, engines growling and mufflers rumbling.

Winston froze. His eyes widened. His ears flattened. Instead of prancing ahead, he backed up and cowered at my feet.

Holding tightly to his leash to keep him from darting into traffic, I dropped to my knees on either side of his trembling body. I wrapped my arms around him, gathered him close, and sheltered him until the terror passed by.

I suspect Winston might have felt a little like Ruth from Moab.

Ruth, the woman after whom the eighth book of the Old Testament was named, was sheltered too. A Moabite who worshipped the god Chemosh, she had married into a Jewish family fleeing famine in Israel. Over time she'd come to believe in the one true God. But along with her sister-in-law and mother-in-law, Naomi, she experienced the terror of widowhood.

After Naomi had buried her husband, and then her two sons, she had no reason to remain in the land of the Moabites. She heard the famine had ended in Israel, so she prepared to return to her native land. Before leaving, she released her first daughter-in-law with a blessing. Then she turned to Ruth. "Your sister-in-law is going back to her people and her gods. Go back with her" (Ruth 1:15).

But Ruth had found no hope in the god of her ancestors. Her husband was dead. She had no children. Deep in her soul she knew—only the God of Israel, Naomi's God, could save her.

"Don't urge me to leave you or to turn back from you," Ruth pleaded. "Where you go I will go, and where you stay I will stay. Your people will be my people and your God my God" (v. 16).

With no means of support and no plan, Ruth followed her heartbroken mother-in-law to the land of Israel. Starvation and desperation forced her to glean in the fields, scrounging for grain behind the reapers. Each night she threshed the small amount of grain she'd gathered, wondering what would become of them and praying for a miracle.

As she labored, she caught the eye of the wealthy landowner, Boaz. "Whose young woman is this?" he asked. A few probing questions revealed Ruth's godly character, behavior, and faith.

"I've been told all about what you have done for your mother-in-law since the death of your husband," he said to her, "how you left your father and mother and your homeland and came to live with a people you did not know before. May the LORD repay you for what you have done. May you be richly rewarded by the LORD, the God of Israel, under whose wings you have come to take refuge" (2:11–12).

As Winston ran to me for protection and refuge when he was afraid, Ruth staked her faith on the God of Israel. What this would involve in her uncertain future, she had no idea, but she was all in. She didn't just believe in the God of Israel, she acted. She flung herself wholly on Him, trusting Him to lead, guide, and provide for her and her mother-in-law.

God sent wise counsel through Naomi.

"My daughter," Naomi said, "I must find a home for you, where you will be well provided for" (3:1). She coached Ruth how to approach Boaz and urged her to ask him to exercise his right as a close kinsman and take her as his wife.

Ruth believed God was leading her through Naomi's advice, so she followed her somewhat strange instructions. (You can read about them in the third chapter of Ruth.) Boaz responded with shocked surprise. "The LORD bless you, my daughter. . . . This kindness is greater than that which you showed earlier: You have not run after the younger men, whether rich or poor. And now, my daughter, don't be afraid. I will do for you all you ask. All the people of my town know that you are a woman of noble character" (vv. 10–11).

Boaz took as his bride the woman he'd come to love and respect. In time, God blessed their relationship with a son. That son became the great-grandfather of King David and the ancestor of Jesus Christ, the Messiah.

Ruth had been "richly rewarded by the Lord, the God of Israel, under whose wings [she had] come to take refuge" (2:12).

No one knows what might have happened to Ruth the Moabite if she hadn't placed her faith in God and run to Him for refuge. We all know what happened because she did.

Winston, in his simple trust, knew to run to me, his owner and protector. Ruth knew to run to almighty God for His help and protection.

As believers, our instincts should be like Winston's and Ruth's—run to the One who has promised never to leave us or forsake us, so we may boldly say, "The Lord is my helper; I will not be afraid. What can mere mortals do to me?" (Hebrews 13:6).

There in His presence may "a full reward be given [us] by the Lord, the God of Israel, under whose wings [we] have come to take **refuge**!" (Ruth 2:12 ESV).

glory

Make models of the tumors and of the rats that are destroying the country, and give glory to Israel's god.

1 Samuel 6:5

I hadn't seen my college friend Samantha in two decades, but one day, there she was—on aisle four of the grocery store, comparing nutrition labels on two cans of soup. We squealed, hugged, and tried to outtalk each other. Knowing we needed to catch up, we agreed to grab a drink at the coffee shop next door before we parted.

As we sipped passion tea and enjoyed the shop's air-conditioning, we updated each other on the last twenty years of our lives. Samantha went first.

"After college I went on to get my master's," she said. "I just happened to hear about an internship—random luck, really, and I got in. After I'd worked with the company for a few years, I met a woman who told me about a doctoral program in Upstate New York.

All that good Karma I'd sown finally came back around, I guess, and I was accepted."

"Maybe it wasn't luck or Karma," I said. "I believe God orders the events of our lives. It sounds to me like He opened some amazing opportunities for you."

"Hmm," she said, raising her straw to her lips. "Maybe."

I thought of our conversation when I stumbled across a highly entertaining and revealing account in 1 Samuel 4–7. The Israelites, under the leadership of the elderly priest, Eli, had been soundly defeated in a battle against their archenemies, the Philistines. Instead of seeking God's direction, they had presumptuously plunged into war, carrying the ark of God—the symbol of God's presence—into battle like a lucky rabbit's foot.

The Philistines routed the Israelites and carried off their national treasure as spoil. They placed the ark in the temple of their god, Dagon, adding the God of Israel to their collection of deities. To the Philistines, the campaign was a rousing success.

Until it wasn't.

They soon discovered that almighty God shares His glory with no one. Strange and horrible things began to happen.

First, God flicked the image of their idol Dagon on its face a few times and broke off body parts. (You can read this humorous account in 1 Samuel 5:1–5.) Then God sent a terrible plague. Like a game of Hot Potato, the leaders passed around the ark of God from town to town trying to stop the scourge of painful sores and tumors that accompanied its presence.

Unlike Egypt's Pharaoh, who, when given the opportunity to free the Israelites from slavery, persisted in his hardheartedness until his nation was destroyed, the Philistine leaders listened to the wise counsel of their priests. They knew they must return the ark of God to Israel, and they must do it reverently. "If you return the ark of the god of Israel," the priests advised, "do not send it back to him without a gift; by all means send a guilt offering to him. Then you will be healed" (6:3).

After much deliberation about what might constitute an acceptable offering, they chose to make gold images of their tumors and the rats that had carried the plague and send them back with the ark.

Weird, huh? But it worked.

Why? Because their reasoning was sound. A powerful God must be treated with respect and honor. "Make models of the tumors and of the rats that are destroying the country," the priests advised, "*and give glory to Israel's god*" (6:5; emphasis added).

Unlike my friend Samantha, these idolaters knew God deserved the glory for the events in their lives.

They acknowledged God's power and control. "When the people of Ashdod saw what was happening, they said, 'The ark of the god of Israel must not stay here with us, because his hand is heavy on us and on Dagon our god'" (5:7).

In contrast, people down through the ages, and even more so today, have credited science, nature, luck, skill, coincidence, and Karma for the world around us and the events of our days.

The Philistines also pointed others to God's greatness. The priests told their leaders, "Why do you harden your hearts as the Egyptians and Pharaoh did? When Israel's god dealt harshly with them, did they not send the Israelites out so they could go on their way?" (6:6). The pagan priests gave God the credit and glory.

Finally, they submitted to God's will. They surrendered their plans to His. The Philistines knew they couldn't keep their treasure. God was more powerful, and His will would prevail.

As Christians, we should be the first to acknowledge God's creative power and control over the affairs of mankind. Jesus reminded the Pharisees of this when he said, "I tell you . . . if they [His disciples] keep quiet, the stones will cry out" (Luke 19:40).

Even as a believer, I struggle with this. I cling to my agenda and my plans and refuse to surrender to God's superior wisdom. I glorify my plans above His. Sometimes He has to pry my hands off something I value because I won't release it.

I've come to realize my unwillingness to yield is really just a front for my lack of trust—not believing that God is as glorious in all His ways as He truly is. I don't treat Him as worthy of my obedience. I fail to give Him the glory He's due.

How ironic that God chose to use a city full of pagan idolaters to teach us how to give God glory. Sadly, although the Philistines acknowledged God's control, pointed others to His greatness, and submitted to His will, they never took the final step and surrendered their hearts and lives to Him. As best we can tell from Scripture, the Philistines remained estranged from God.

Thankfully, we can learn from them. God graciously calls to us to look around at all He has created and all He's doing and acknowledge Him as Lord. We can begin today, as I did with my friend Samantha, to point others to His greatness as we submit to His plan for our lives.

In this way, we honor God as Lord of all and give Him **glory**.

worshipped

He went into the house of the LORD and worshiped.

2 Samuel 12:20

My husband, David, and I had been planning our youth group's mission trip to Cabo San Lucas, Mexico, for more than a year. We'd navigated the waters of international travel, customs, and transportation; eaten our first authentic Mexican meal; and awakened after a blessed night's sleep. We were finally here.

Our first full day in Cabo would be filled with cultural encounters in the marketplace. "We want you to experience the sights and sounds of Mexico before you jump into ministry," our hosts said. Carlos and Sandy were church planters preparing for a fifty-person missions conference. Our team would prepare meals and run the youth program.

Shopping is different in Mexico, where every price is negotiable and every purchase open to haggling. I'd taken the girls to buy souvenirs while David took the guys to an auto shop to get equipment we'd need that week.

I was arms deep in multicolored blankets when Sandy's cell phone rang.

"What? Who?" she said, her forehead wrinkling in concern. "We'll be right home."

Sandy turned toward me. "A call came in from the States," she said. "There's been an emergency with one of your family members. The connection was poor. Our daughter couldn't get the details."

Even now, more than a decade later, my stomach clenches with the paralyzing fear that gripped me when I heard those words.

Who could it be? Did Dad have another heart attack? Was someone injured in a car wreck? Did something happen to my sister Cindy?

Cindy had been in the hospital for several weeks. We'd debated about whether I should accompany David on the trip, but doctors had assured us her condition was stable.

Racing back to Carlos and Sandy's house to use their landline, we called every family member who might know something. After ten terrifying minutes, we finally reached someone who could tell us what happened.

My sister was fine, but David's was not.

Kay had suffered a triple brain aneurysm. Doctors had placed her on life support while they assessed the damage.

Two days later she died.

When we received the news, we stumbled to our room, crumpled to the floor, and wept. Gut-wrenching, heartrending wails emanated from places too deep for words.

All we could see in our mind's eye was Kay's crooked smile. All we could hear were her last words: "I'm proud of you, Brother." We couldn't believe we'd never see her again on this earth.

When my husband's sobs quieted, he said, in a voice thick with trust and faith, "The LORD gave, and the LORD has taken away. Blessed be the name of the LORD" (Job 1:21 NKJV).

Worship seems like an unlikely friend of grief, but it can be the most welcome of comforters.

The book of 2 Samuel reveals another David drowning in an ocean of grief. Seven days earlier, King David's infant son had fallen gravely ill. Day and night David had stretched prostrate on the ground, fasting and pleading with God to spare his child's life.

On the eighth day, servants brought the news no parent should ever receive—his tiny son was dead.

The finality of the baby's death must have sucked the air from David's lungs and the hope from his future. All the dreams he'd had for his son would be buried alongside the tiny body that had just begun to live.

In moments like these, when the tragedies of life defy our under-standing and threaten to drown our faith, we cling to the anchor of God's character. God's Word reminds us our heavenly Father does not willingly cause grief (Lamentations 3:33). He is near to the bro-kenhearted (Psalm 34:18). He sees each one of our tears (56:8). He bears our sorrows and identifies with our grief (Isaiah 53:4). Our suffering is never pointless (Romans 8:28).

Focusing on what they knew to be true about God—that He was loving, kind, and good—allowed both Davids to come to God in their grief. To pour out their pain. To stake their trust in their heav-enly Father and acknowledge that when they didn't understand His ways, they could trust His heart.

"Then David got up from the ground. After he had washed, put on lotions and changed his clothes, he went into the house of the Lord and worshiped" (2 Samuel 12:20).

"Can I bring him back again?" David asked his servants when they questioned his behavior. "I will go to him, but he will not re-turn to me" (v. 23).

By choosing to worship God, King David received God's comfort. One day he would spend eternity in the presence of God—with his son. My David experienced the same comfort. As he worshipped, he was reminded that because Kay had trusted in Christ, he'd see her again, healthy and whole, in the presence of Jesus.

Tears are cathartic. Grief is necessary. But worship is crucial. For King David and my David, true healing began when they fell on their faces and **worshipped**.

questions

When the queen of Sheba heard about the fame
of Solomon and his relationship to the LORD,
she came to test Solomon with hard questions.

1 Kings 10:1

I wasn't your typical high school senior—carefree, confident, ready
to take on the world. I embraced a more mindful and cautious approach. I worked hard, took my education seriously, and struggled
to make decisions.

As my future stretched before me—a vast expanse of gloriously
frightening possibilities—I knew the decisions I'd make in the next
few years would chart the course of my life. The options swirled re-
lentlessly in my head, churning the waters of my mind and making
me feel anxious and queasy.

*Where should I go to college? What should I study? Where should I live?
Who should I date? Who should I marry? Where does God fit into all this?*

I'd fall asleep imagining endless scenarios and awaken with the
weight of confusion sitting like a suitcase on my chest. I longed to

open the case and don the future that was right for me, but I didn't know how.

I needed wisdom greater than what I possessed. Where could I find it?

The queen of Sheba and I have a lot in common. We both had lots of questions and few answers.

"When the queen of Sheba heard about the fame of Solomon and his relationship to the LORD, she came to test Solomon with hard questions" (1 Kings 10:1).

The Bible doesn't tell us much about the mysterious monarch who appears and disappears in the tenth chapter of 1 Kings, but what we know is impressive. Rich, influential, and intellectually curious, the queen had heard about Solomon's God and the wisdom God had bestowed on him. She wanted to know more. She had big issues tumbling around in her heart, and she was willing to do whatever necessary to find the answers.

So she filled her ancient Samsonites with gold, jewels, and spices from the royal treasury, summoned her camel driver, and organized the first caravan headed north. "She came to Solomon and talked with him about all that she had on her mind" (v. 2).

Like the camel-riding queen, I took my questions to a man who knew God—my pastor.

He met with me one summer afternoon and told me God is the ultimate source of wisdom. If I didn't have a personal relationship with Him, I'd continue to stumble in the darkness of my confusion and limited knowledge. He affirmed what I already knew—I needed someone bigger and wiser than myself to direct my life.

My pastor explained to me that when people repent of their sin and surrender their lives to God, the Holy Spirit comes to live in them (1 Corinthians 3:16). John 16:13 tells us the Spirit will "guide [us] into all truth."

Although God imparted supernatural wisdom to Solomon, Christians can access the same wisdom by reading, studying, and memorizing the Bible. We find Solomon's inspired words in three books—Proverbs, Ecclesiastes, and Song of Songs—but we can gain godly wisdom from every book of the Bible.

"All Scripture is God-breathed," 2 Timothy 3:16–17 tells us, "and is useful for teaching, rebuking, correcting and training in righteousness, so that the servant of God may be thoroughly equipped for every good work."

As I grew in my relationship with God and learned to study the Bible, meditate on it, and apply it to my life, my wisdom grew. I became more confident about making decisions and learned to seek God's direction and will for my life.

The queen of Sheba brought her questions to a man who knew God, and I did too. Thousands of years apart, we discovered a universal truth—God is the source for all the answers to life's hard **questions**.

died

> Now Elisha had been suffering from the illness
> from which he died.
>
> *2 Kings 13:14*

"I am very sad," my friend Justin wrote in a text message. "My pastor's earthly pilgrimage is about to come to an end. His cancer is now untreatable, and he has gone home to be with his family before his ultimate homegoing."

He went on to share how his godly pastor had impacted him and many others. "This man has poured into my life and the lives of his congregation for forty years. Only heaven will reveal how God has used him."

King Joash didn't have the benefit of MRI scans and biopsies, but he may have suspected Elisha the prophet, his counselor and spiritual guide, was gravely ill. Scripture confirms this: "Now Elisha had been suffering from the illness from which he died" (2 Kings 13:14).

Somehow, this doesn't seem right. Godly men and women should live forever. I still mourn evangelist Billy Graham's death, even though he was ninety-nine years old when he died. How could God take someone away who has been such a hero, defender, and champion for the cause of Christ? Especially now, when the world needs men like him to guide and influence us?

The sad fact is that everyone must die. Even mighty men of God. Even us.

Yet even as they die, we can learn from them. Men like Justin's pastor, Elisha, and Billy Graham teach us how to die well. As we study how they lived and died, we see three distinguishing characteristics:

They trusted God with the timing of their deaths. Although we may see a death as "premature," Scripture reminds us, "All the days ordained for me were written in your book before one of them came to be" (Psalm 139:16). We can trust God to accomplish His good work in and through us before He takes us home. He leaves no deed undone and no mission unfulfilled.

From the senior saint who dies at ninety-nine to the unborn baby who died before he took his first breath, each life accomplishes what God intended for it. We can say with confidence, as Justin's pastor did in a Facebook post following his cancer diagnosis, "We are trusting the Lord for His purpose."

They trusted God with the details of their deaths. When we face a life-threatening diagnosis, experience a devastating accident, or endure the increasingly challenging effects of aging, it's easy to feel frightened. We hear stories of excruciating chemotherapy regimens and wonder if we'll suffer a similar torture. We listen to news reports of people who died in tornadoes, floods, or crime sprees, and we grow anxious. We know death comes to all, and some nights we lie awake imagining what our own departure will look like.

Men and women of God can know that the same God who has walked beside them every day of their lives will also walk beside them as they die. He will not abandon them. Isaiah 46:4 reminds us, "Even to your old age and gray hairs I am he, I am he who will sustain you. I have made you and I will carry you." Whatever death we face, we won't face it alone. God will be by our sides.

They trusted God enough to share the reason for their hope. Believers in Jesus Christ can spend their lives seeking ways to glorify God and draw others to Him. As the end of their lives near, their approaching deaths grant them new ways to bring God glory and point others to Him.

If you've ever seen a Christian die full of faith, you know this is true. Instead of railing against God in bitterness and anger, they surrender their wills to His and embrace every divine opportunity to share the reason for the hope that lies within them (1 Peter 3:15). They witness to loved ones, write emails to distant friends, and share their faith with doctors, nurses, and caregivers. Capturing every fleeting day, they boldly share Jesus with all who will listen.

Whether a terminal illness like Elisha's ends our lives or we die of old age like Graham, we can use each day's circumstances to impact those around us for God's kingdom. As Graham said, "Heaven doesn't make this life less important; it makes it more important."[1]

I'm not sure when Elisha entered heaven, but Graham stepped through the portal between this world and the next on February 21, 2018. He prepared the world for his passing by saying, "Someday you will read or hear that Billy Graham is dead. Don't you believe a word of it. I shall be more alive than I am now. I will just have changed my address. I will have gone into the presence of God."[2]

Embracing the living hope that surrounds us, Graham left us with an inspired glimpse beyond the veil. "Death for the Christian is the doorway to heaven's glory. Because of Christ's resurrection we can joyously say with Paul, 'Where, O death, is your victory?'"[3]

Whether we have an "official" diagnosis or we're enjoying good health, each of us has an illness that will one day lead to death—our own humanity. Let's live each day mindful of the legacy we want to leave behind and the legacy we hope to take with us into eternity. May we glorify God by the way we lived and the way we **died**.

consult

[The Levites] may bring up the ark of the Lord God of Israel. . . .
For because you did not do it the first time,
the Lord our God broke out against us,
because we did not consult Him about the proper order.

1 Chronicles 15:13 NKJV

During the nine months I carried our first child, I bought at least ten books on pregnancy and childbirth. During the thirty-plus years of parenting that have followed, I've probably borrowed a hundred more on topics such as birth order, sibling rivalry, learning styles, personality types, proper nutrition, healthy lifestyles, self-esteem, and discipleship.

I discovered that being pregnant, giving birth, and caring for an infant feel like frolicking through flowery meadows compared with the Ironman Triathlon of parenting a child to adulthood.

My husband and I quickly realized how little we knew about raising children. We knew we needed help, so we consulted those whose wisdom and experience exceeded ours. We sought out men and women who knew God and His Word and how to apply biblical principles to life. They became our most helpful resources. They taught us, first-generation Christian parents, how to find answers to our parenting (and life) questions in God's Word.

We discovered when we sought wise counsel and studied the Bible for insight and direction, we made better decisions. King David discovered this too.

As the new king of Israel, David determined to bring the ark of the covenant to Jerusalem. Saul, his predecessor, had neglected this precious symbol of God's presence, leaving it in Kiriath Jearim, a city nine miles outside Jerusalem. Unfortunately, David allowed his zeal for the project to chart the course of his actions. He gathered Israel around him, staged a procession, and charged in like an eight-year-old Boy Scout in a parade.

At David's instructions, Uzzah, one of the king's muscle men, loaded the precious vessel onto a cart and off they went. The ox stumbled, the ark slid, and Uzzah reached out to steady the ark. The procession came to a screeching halt when God struck Uzzah dead.

Shocked and frightened, David deposited the ark at the first house he came to and hightailed it back to Jerusalem to sulk.

Because he was a man after God's own heart, it didn't take him long to realize God never acts capriciously. If God took a man's life, it was for good reason. David wasn't sure what that reason was, but he was determined to find out.

His search led him to God's Word, the source of all wisdom. When he consulted the priests and the ancient text we now know as the book of Leviticus, he discovered God had given specific instructions for transporting the ark. Had he sought God's direction first, he would have gained the knowledge he needed to accomplish his mission safely and reverently.

Similarly, God has "given us everything we need for a godly life through our knowledge of him who called us by his own glory and goodness" (2 Peter 1:3). Whether we're navigating the waters of parenting, making business decisions, or working through difficult interpersonal relationships, God's Word provides the timeless truths and wisdom we need. Godly counsel gives us better understanding of His Word to help us make wise decisions. Prayer leads us before the throne of grace with boldness to receive help and insight from the Holy Spirit.

As He did for King David, God has provided everything we need to navigate this challenging journey called life. I'm grateful His supply of wisdom never runs out. Whether we seek instruction in parenting, relationships, business, or any other area, we'll make wise decisions when we learn, as David did, to make God the first one we **consult**.

stand

And from all their territories the priests and the Levites who were in all Israel took their stand with [Rehoboam].

2 Chronicles 11:13 NKJV

Dick had tormented his roommate, Bob, for four years. He'd mocked Bob's faith and his belief in the Bible. Dick's analytical mind found Bob's unswerving belief in Scripture maddening and foolish.

One Saturday toward the end of their senior year, two coeds visiting from a local church knocked on their door and invited Dick to church.

So he went.

At the close of the service, the pastor shared a simple gospel invitation. Although Bob had shared the gospel with him often, this time something within him stirred. He called the office the following day and made an appointment to talk with the pastor. At the end of their meeting, Dick surrendered his life to Christ.

"I couldn't imagine how a simple prayer of faith and surrender could change anything," he remembered, "but it did." The Spirit of God now lived inside him.

Eager to share his newfound faith, he told his classmates he'd become a Christian.

"You actually believe that stuff about God creating the world, and a man getting swallowed by a whale, and the earth being destroyed by a flood?" one guy asked him.

"I hadn't thought about it until that moment," Dick recounted later, "but I knew I had to take a stand."

"Yes," he said with conviction and a touch of surprise. "I do."

Second Chronicles tells of men like Dick who stood for truth despite opposition.

King Solomon was dead, and his son Rehoboam took the throne. His reign didn't start or end well, but God had promised David (Rehoboam's grandfather) that he'd always have a descendent on the throne. He wouldn't completely remove His hand of blessing from the kingly line. Despite Rehoboam's foolish choices, God allowed him to govern the territories of Judah and Benjamin, including Jerusalem—the city of David and the place where God's temple stood.

Meanwhile Jeroboam, the leader of the Northern Kingdom, dove headlong into idolatry and dragged the Israelites with him. He rejected the Levites who served as priests for the one true God and threw in his lot with the idolatrous nations surrounding them. Since the temple of God was in Rehoboam's kingdom, Jeroboam created places for his people to worship and "appointed his own priests for the high places and for the goat and calf idols he had made" (2 Chronicles 11:15).

God's faithful priests skedaddled out of Israel and down to God's true temple as fast as their sandaled feet could go.

"The priests and Levites from all their districts throughout Israel sided with him [Rehoboam]. The Levites even abandoned their pasturelands and property and came to Judah and Jerusalem, because

Jeroboam and his sons had rejected them as priests of the LORD" (vv. 13–14).

The Levites weren't the only ones strapping on their sandals and hightailing it south. "Those from every tribe of Israel who set their hearts on seeking the LORD, the God of Israel, followed the Levites to Jerusalem to offer sacrifices to the LORD, the God of their ancestors" (v. 16).

Their exodus seemed foolish to many because King Jeroboam ruled from a position of political, military, and financial strength. He governed ten of the twelve tribes of Israel and controlled their armies, resources, and land. King Rehoboam governed only two measly tribes. He occupied land half the size of Israel. To align themselves with Judah and King Rehoboam, the Levites and other Israelites had to forsake their homes, possessions, and land.

But to stay with Jeroboam, they'd have to forsake God.

Joshua had thrown down the gauntlet generations before. "Choose for yourselves this day whom you will serve, whether the gods your ancestors served . . . or the gods . . . in whose land you are living. But as for me and my household, we will serve the LORD" (Joshua 24:15).

The Levites and those who set their hearts to seek the God of Israel remembered Joshua's words. More important, they remembered God's promise to bless them as long as they remained loyal to Him.

Dick's decision to stand with God and defend His Word was an important step in his Christian life. In the fifty years since, he's had to choose again and again whether he'll ride the river of popular culture or swim upstream against the current. Like the Levites of Rehoboam's day, Dick's courage and commitment have inspired generations of Christ followers. He challenges them to know what they believe, own what they believe, and, when necessary, take a **stand**.

fast

There, by the Ahava Canal, I proclaimed a fast, so that we might
humble ourselves before our God and ask him for a safe journey
for us and our children, with all our possessions.

Ezra 8:21

Desperation drives a person to fast.

I know. I've been desperate. And I've fasted.

I've fasted when heart-stopping fear clutched my chest. I've gone
without food when swirling confusion overwhelmed me. I've ab-
stained from meals as I entreated God to protect and preserve my
loved ones. And I've forsaken physical food in exchange for spiritual
food.

Even though the Bible mentions fasting more than seventy
times, we seldom hear about it. When was the last time your pastor
preached on fasting?

The practice of going without food for a specific period of time to
seek God appears in both the Old Testament and the New. Heroes
of the faith fasted. Kings fasted. Jesus fasted.

Lest you think (or hope) the practice of fasting is an ancient ritual that disappeared with the old covenant, you'll discover Jesus assumed in Matthew 6:16–17 that his disciples (we) would fast. "When [not if] you fast, . . ." he said.

Ezra the priest modeled the timeless practice of fasting.

God had tasked Ezra with the responsibility of leading a group of exiles back to Israel after seventy years of captivity in Babylon. In addition to shepherding men, women, and children across almost 1,700 miles of treacherous territory, he also had a great quantity of gold and silver to take with him, given to him by King Cyrus.

Imagine traveling halfway across the southwestern United States on foot with toddlers, old people, and everyone in between, carrying gold bars in your backpacks. No hotels, no buses, no roadside restaurants. Only sand, camels, and rough terrain.

Overwhelmed with the enormity of the assignment and its inherent dangers, Ezra knew not to set out without seeking God. "There, by the Ahava Canal, I proclaimed a fast, so that we might humble ourselves before our God and ask him for a safe journey for us and our children, with all our possessions" (Ezra 8:21).

The Israelites deprived themselves of food not to bargain with God for a favor, but to demonstrate the seriousness of their plea and sharpen their spiritual senses. By removing the distraction of food, they were better able to seek and sense the Lord's direction.

"So we fasted and petitioned our God about this, and he answered our prayer" (v. 23). God gave Ezra wisdom to organize the caravan. Then He surrounded it with His protection. "On the twelfth day of the first month we set out from the Ahava Canal to go to Jerusalem. The hand of our God was on us, and he protected us from enemies and bandits along the way" (v. 31).

I faced a frightening situation years ago. It didn't involve bandits but was no less terrifying. After a long season of trial, one of my friends was drowning in hopelessness. I lived too far away to come to her rescue. I didn't have the power to change her situation.

I couldn't wave a magic wand and fix her circumstances. Only God could restore her hope and protect her from discouragement.

So I set aside a day to fast and pray. From morning until evening, every time I felt a pang of hunger, I talked to God. I asked Him to meet her need according to the riches of His glory. I begged Him to fill her heart with hope and courage and a will to live. I pleaded with Him to send believers into her life who could speak words of truth to her. And most of all, I prayed for His mercy.

Toward the end of the day, my spiritual burden lifted and peace soothed my anxious heart. I spoke aloud a final prayer of surrender and ended my fast.

Later that evening I received a phone call. "God spoke to me through a stranger today," my friend said. "She reminded me that God sees my situation and cares about my needs. I feel much better. I knew you'd want to know."

Desperation drives us to fast and pray. When we humble ourselves, admit our need, and cast our burdens on God, He meets us there. By depriving ourselves of our basic need for food in order to seek His face and understand His will, we say to God, "I want your power to be released into this situation more than I want food in my stomach. I need to be more spiritually alive than physically alive."

This is the kind of faith God rewards. In response to our pleas, He reveals His will to us. He speaks to our hearts. He rids us (at least for a time) of our tendency to choose comfort over commitment, and frees us to rest in Him.

Ezra knew (and I have learned) that fasting isn't a quid pro quo exchange where we give up food to manipulate God to answer our prayers. It's a faith-filled action that says to God, "I want your will to be done in this situation more than I want my own comfort."

God ordained fasting for times when we need an extra measure of wisdom, direction, and power. I'm grateful He gave us a means to bare our hearts to Him and wait in humble submission. This is His intent when He calls believers to **fast**.

zealously

Next to him, Baruch son of Zabbai zealously repaired
another section, from the angle to the entrance
of the house of Eliashib the high priest.

Nehemiah 3:20

When I arrived at church at 5 a.m. to pray in the prayer room, Sandy McPherson was already there. He'd started the coffee pot, turned on the lights, and pulled his cleaning cart out of the utility closet.

"Good morning, Mrs. Lori," he called. "This is the day the Lord has made. Let us rejoice and be glad in it!" When I left an hour later, he was rubbing the handrails with wood polish and humming the tune to "Amazing Grace."

I returned to church that night for a Bible study. One woman, overwhelmed by the stress of caring for her aging parents, burst into tears toward the end of our meeting. We let her cry, commiserated, and took turns praying for her. It was after nine o'clock when we left the building.

Glancing back, I saw Sandy switch off the lights and lock the door behind him. He walked toward his ancient Honda parked at the back of the lot. The whistled notes of "Victory in Jesus" wafted behind him.

When the local Christian magazine I worked for gave me the opportunity to spotlight someone who exemplified dedication and joyful service, I chose Sandy.

Sitting across the table from him in the church's coffee shop, I got right to the point. "Sandy, I've never seen you without a smile on your face. You work circles around people forty years younger than you, and you do the most menial tasks with joy. What's the secret to your great attitude?"

He fidgeted with his napkin, folding and unfolding it like a fan. Clearly uncomfortable with the attention, he tugged at the neck of his T-shirt.

"Mrs. Lori, I love working here. Before God saved me, I was nothin'. Then He lifted me up out of the miry clay, set my feet upon a rock, and put a new song in my mouth. It's an honor and a privilege to serve Him in His house."

I thought of Sandy when I learned about Baruch son of Zabbai in Nehemiah 3. The Israelites' seventy-year captivity in Babylon had ended, and Ezra the priest had returned to Jerusalem with a number of exiles. They'd rebuilt the temple, but the wall around the city lay in ruins.

God sent Nehemiah to challenge them to rebuild the wall and secure their city. "You see the trouble we are in," he said. "Jerusalem lies in ruins, and its gates have been burned with fire. Come, let us rebuild the wall of Jerusalem, and we will no longer be in disgrace" (Nehemiah 2:17).

"Let us start rebuilding," the people responded. "So they began this good work" (v. 18).

The following chapter contains a long list of the names of those who made the repairs. Joiada made repairs. Zadok made repairs.

Meremoth made repairs. The men of Eliashib made repairs. Faithful men fulfilled their duty and did their part, much like we do when we sign up for a shift in the nursery or take a turn mowing the church yard.

But Baruch's name stands out. "Next to him, Baruch son of Zabbai *zealously* repaired another section, from the angle to the entrance of the house of Eliashib the high priest" (3:20; emphasis mine).

Baruch didn't just do his duty. He worked *zealously*. The Hebrew word for "zealously," *hārâ*, means to glow or grow warm; or, figuratively, to blaze up.[4] Baruch was *on fire* for the Lord. He worked with passion and enthusiasm, building his section of the wall, right next to the house of the high priest—the minister of God.

Baruch understood that his work, though menial, mattered. His contribution would help God's ministers and enable God's work to continue. This awareness brought energy to his labor and joy to his heart.

This thought should do the same for us. Instead of just fulfilling an obligation, we should recognize that working for God is a privilege and a delight. Like Sandy, our hearts should glow with gratitude and shine brightly enough that others notice and glorify God.

Baruch and Sandy remind me that nothing I do in God's name and for God's people is insignificant. God sees and delights in our zeal.

How do I know? Because God saw Baruch's zealous labor and commended it in the canon of Scripture. "Baruch . . . zealously repaired another section" (v. 20).

Hebrews 6:10 affirms God's heart toward those who labor enthusiastically in His name: "God is not unjust; he will not forget your work and the love you have shown him as you have helped his people and continue to help them."

Whether God calls us to trim bushes or lead a Bible study, may we follow Baruch's and Sandy's examples and do our work faithfully, joyfully, and **zealously**.

favor

The king loved Esther more than all the women, and she won
grace and favor in his sight more than all the virgins.

Esther 2:17 ESV

I've always imagined that great victories come about because of great
battles. That heroes ride in on white steeds. That deliverance comes
through Avenger-type muscle men with superpowers or brilliant-
minded women savvy in the ways of the world.

God, however, uses unlikely people to accomplish extraordinary
feats. Esther is one of these people. A teenager living in exile in
Babylon, her government upended her life when officials snatched
her up. She became one of the many young women competing to
become the next queen.

When I was fifteen years old, my parents decided it was time for
our family to move. I'll never forget their announcement. As soon as
my sisters and I completed the school year, they'd put our house on
the market, and we'd leave Rhode Island forever.

I grew up in the sleepy seaside town of Bristol, on the shores of Narragansett Bay. My hometown boasts a total area of 20.6 square miles. Ten miles of land; ten miles of water. My sisters and I walked, rode bikes, and took the bus wherever we wanted to go. We were happy and safe.

We'd be moving one thousand miles away to my father's hometown of Columbia, South Carolina. Like Esther, I'd be ripped from my home and carried off to a land far different from my own. Strange foods. Unfamiliar faces. A peculiar dialect. Columbia was landlocked, one hundred miles from the ocean and known for its suffocating heat and humidity.

The day my childhood home went on the market, my friend Jodie and I sat outside and threw rocks at the For Sale sign. We wept. We raged. We plotted my escape. "As soon as I'm eighteen," I vowed, "I'll come back, and I'll never leave again."

I'm sure Esther wept too. But she didn't allow the devastating circumstances of her life to make her bitter. Despite her broken heart, she rose to the challenge of living in a foreign place among pagan people. And God's favor rested upon her.

As she clung to the only thing she had left—her heritage as a child of the Most High God, God gave her grace to shine like a light in a dark place. Her gentle spirit, respectful attitude, and commitment to God set her apart from all the others. God moved in the hearts of those in authority over her, helped her maintain her integrity, and granted her favor.

"Now the young woman [Esther] pleased him, and she obtained his [the eunuch's] favor" (Esther 2:9 NKJV).

God doesn't deliver us out of every difficult circumstance, but He promises to reward the faith we exercise in those circumstances. He blesses us with divine favor to accomplish His purposes through (not despite) the challenges He allows.

"Let love and faithfulness never leave you; bind them around your neck, write them on the tablet of your heart. Then you will win favor and a good name in the sight of God and man" (Proverbs 3:3–4).

As Esther trusted God despite the tragic circumstances of her life, she saw God work in amazing ways. Her gentle respect toward those around her caused her to obtain "the favor of everyone who saw her" (Esther 2:15).

When the time came for her to appear before the king, "the king loved Esther more than all the other women, and she obtained grace and favor in his sight more than all the virgins; so he set the royal crown upon her head and made her queen instead of Vashti" (v. 17 NKJV).

But Esther's coronation wasn't the end of God's favor. He had a greater purpose.

The greatest test of Esther's divine favor arose when wicked Haman tricked the king into signing an edict to annihilate the Jews. Although the king's bodyguards could kill her for approaching King Xerxes to beg for mercy, Esther determined to go before him.

Three days of prayer and fasting bolstered her quaking heart. God had preserved and protected her thus far. He had surrounded her with His goodness and positioned her for this request. She prayed He would see her through. Regardless of the outcome, she would trust Him.

Esther donned her royal robes, gathered her courage, and entered the throne room. Taking a deep breath, she fixed her eyes on the king and surrendered her fate to the King of Kings.

"When he saw Queen Esther standing in the court, he was pleased with her and held out to her the gold scepter that was in his hand. So Esther approached and touched the tip of the scepter" (5:2).

Esther's courageous act ultimately secured deliverance for the Jews and an ironic death to wicked Haman. (Read about it in Esther 7:1–10.)

Like Esther, we often find ourselves neck-deep in circumstances we wouldn't have chosen. The twists and turns of life send us on detours to dark places and difficult seasons. Sickness, divorce, unemployment, and strained relationships exile us from the people and places we hold most dear, and we grieve their loss. We struggle to imagine how God can bring good out of such wretched misery.

And yet He does. He fans into flame the ashes of our former life, refines and restores us, and uses our trust to bring deliverance for ourselves and those around us.

I was convinced, at age fifteen, that my good life was ending. Plucked from my home and sent a thousand miles away, I couldn't imagine how anything positive could come from such a devastating event. But God's favor was upon me.

He connected me with friends who knew Jesus. They welcomed me into their lives and shared Christ with me. In time, God drew my mother and sisters to faith in Jesus Christ too.

When we sold our home and journeyed south, my parents promised us a new home. I never imagined that we'd not only find a physical home, we'd also discover a spiritual home that will never be taken away.

If you're struggling to trust God because life has taken you in a direction you never imagined—or wanted—commit your life to Him. Walk in faith and trust. Then watch how He surrounds you with His **favor**.

happiness

My eyes will never see happiness again.

Job 7:7

"When my wife died," John said one day during a GriefShare meeting, "my joy died with her."

Sarah, a thin woman with kind eyes nodded. Tucking a gray strand of hair behind her ear, she cleared her throat, then spoke. "Ben and I had been married for forty-nine years. We were planning our fiftieth anniversary trip to Hawaii. He died in a car accident two months before the trip. I cried every day for four months."

Kate, the newest member of the group and thirty years their junior, hadn't said a word, but Sarah's honest confession stirred something within her.

"It's been three months since we found Ollie floating in the deep end of the pool," she whispered. She raised her eyes to meet Sarah's sympathetic gaze, then lowered them again as two shiny streams ran down her cheeks.

"When he died, I felt like the sun stopped shining. I'd walk past his bedroom expecting to see him sitting on the floor playing with his Legos. Or I'd be in the grocery store and think, *I need to buy grapes. Ollie loves grapes.* I'd call everyone to the dinner table, 'Jason, Micah, Ollie!'"

She raised her head, saw their nods, then lowered it. "I don't think I'll ever smile again." She covered her face with her hands and sobbed.

Like John, Sarah, and Kate, Job was a good person. He loved his family and served God. When a series of tragedies robbed him of his wealth, his health, and his ten children, he staggered under the bone-crushing weight of his grief.

In his sorrow, he cursed the day he was born. "Why did I not perish at birth, and die as I came from the womb? . . . Or why was I not hidden in the ground like a stillborn child, like an infant who never saw the light of day?" (Job 3:11, 16). "What I feared has come upon me; what I dreaded has happened to me," he said. "I have no peace, no quietness; I have no rest, but only turmoil" (vv. 25–26).

As his grief intensified, he couldn't eat. He couldn't sleep. When he did fall asleep, terrifying nightmares disturbed his rest. He felt as though his suffering would never ease. He longed for the release of death. "My eyes will never see happiness again," he told his friends as he plunged into deep despair (7:7).

When Kate's sobs had quieted, Sarah spoke again. "I don't remember most of what people said to me in the days after Ben died, but one conversation stands out. A friend dropped by to visit. She'd lost her seventeen-year-old son to suicide several years before.

"'Right now,' she said, 'you feel like you'll never be happy again. And certainly never laugh. But you will. And when it happens, don't feel guilty about it. Receive it as a gift from God. Laughter won't discredit Ben or his memory. Happiness won't minimize the loss you feel. It will remind you that your heart still beats. That God is sustaining you. That He's healing your broken heart . . . and will one day restore your joy.'

"I didn't believe it at the time," Sarah said, "but she was right. One afternoon I was watching the neighbor's kittens wrestle around on the back porch. One fell off and rolled all the way down the stairs. The look on its face when it landed tickled me, and I burst into laughter. I thought about how much Ben loved animals, and how he would have loved to see those kittens play, and I laughed some more. Then I cried. But they were good tears."

The Bible tells us God restored Job's joy too. "All his brothers and sisters and everyone who had known him before came and ate with him in his house. They comforted and consoled him over all the trouble the LORD had brought on him. . . . The LORD blessed the latter part of Job's life more than the former part" (42:11–12).

If you or someone you love is grieving today, take comfort from the life of Job. Or perhaps you're mourning something else—a lost job, a relationship, or a dream. Take heart from the psalmist's promise, "Weeping may stay for the night, but rejoicing comes in the morning" (Psalm 30:5).

One day soon, your spirits will lift, your eyes will smile, and your heart will again know **happiness**.

content

But I have calmed and quieted myself, I am like a weaned child
with its mother; like a weaned child I am content.

Psalm 131:2

Holding eight-month-old Collin while he slept was a rare and exquisite treat. The youngest of four siblings, this active little fella usually naps in the car, the stroller, or in his mama's arms. I seldom have the opportunity to rock him to sleep.

I'm not good at juggling the needs of his elder siblings (and keeping them from destroying the house), so when Collin gets sleepy, I usually lay him down in the Pack n' Play, give him a pat, and tiptoe out of the room.

But this Friday my husband was home to oversee the older kids, and I had the pleasure of rocking Collin.

"He almost fell asleep in the swing," my husband told me, handing him over. "Poor little buddy. He can barely keep his eyes open."

I gathered him close and eased into my favorite rocking chair. If you've ever held a breastfed baby to your chest, you know they often root around seeking milk—whether you're their mama or not. If their hunger isn't satisfied, boy, are they mad. They thrash. They kick. They scream. They're not happy, and the whole neighborhood knows it.

But Collin's belly was full. His mama had nursed him before she left, and he'd snacked on strawberries, banana, and tiny bites of pancake with his sisters and brother. He drifted off peacefully as I held him close, tucked in the crook of my arm.

Psalm 131:2 reminds us that we, too, can rest in contentment and security. "But I have calmed and quieted myself," David the psalmist wrote, "I am like a weaned child with its mother; like a weaned child I am content."

David rested contentedly like a weaned child in the arms of his Savior because he trusted Him. He had no need to thrash about, fearful God couldn't or wouldn't take care of him. In David's spiritual infancy, God had provided everything he needed. Now, with his stomach (and his heart) full of God's goodness, he could rest in quiet confidence.

This tiny psalm, the third shortest in the Bible, tells us how David developed that peaceful trust.

First, he approached God humbly. "My heart is not proud, LORD, my eyes are not haughty" (v. 1). Humble Christians recognize that every breath we take, every day we live, and every opportunity that comes our way falls from the hands of our benevolent Father. Instead of approaching Him like a spoiled child demanding our way, we come before God as a grateful son or daughter. In confidence and trust, we submit to His will and trust His heart.

Second, David accepted that he'd never fully understand God's will or His way. "I do not concern myself with great matters or things too wonderful for me" (v. 1). David knew God's mind contained the knowledge of the universe. The creative genius of a master artist. The infinite wisdom of the ages. Unlike those who refuse to put their faith in God until they get all their questions answered, a restful believer accepts by faith what we don't understand.

"As the heavens are higher than the earth, so are my ways higher than your ways and my thoughts than your thoughts" (Isaiah 55:9).

Just as Collin slept in my arms, we can climb into the strong arms of God and calm our hearts. No thrashing. No kicking. No screaming. We can rest confident and **content**.

builds

The wise woman builds her house, but with her own hands
the foolish one tears hers down.

Proverbs 14:1

A friend from high school almost burned her house down a few years ago.

Not intentionally, but she struck the match that lit the candle that caught the curtains on fire while she slept, eventually engulfing the house in flames.

In God's mercy, she awakened to discover the fire. She screamed for her husband and daughters, who were sleeping upstairs, and they escaped. They weren't injured, but she suffered minor burns. Their house was destroyed.

I talked with her after the fire. She looked at me with eyes still haunted by the horror of that night.

"Sometimes I have nightmares of what could have happened," she said, a sob catching in her throat. She studied her hands, still burned and bandaged. "I could have destroyed my home . . . and my family . . . with my own hands."

Proverbs 14:1 describes a similar scenario: "The wise woman builds her house, but with her own hands the foolish one tears hers down."

Pulls it down. With her own hands.

My friend never intended to damage her house or endanger her family, yet her actions brought about great destruction. Similarly, many of us tear down our homes without even realizing it. Piece by piece. Stone by stone. Section by section.

How?

Here are four common ways.

Criticism. Critical words poke holes in tender souls. When we emphasize the negative and fail to recognize the positive, we wound families, marriages, and friendships.

Instead of celebrating progress, a critical spirit focuses on everything that isn't perfect and everyone who falls short of its expectations. It fails to recognize the value of honest efforts, loving gestures, or kind deeds.

Those we love find the pressure of an impossible standard too heavy to bear. They grow weary of trying and falling short time after time. Sometimes they stop trying altogether. A critical person tears down their house with their own hands.

Comparison. Comparison assigns value to what we possess based on what someone else has. You have a kind, sweet husband? She has a kind sweet husband who leads family devotions and prays with her every night before she falls asleep. You and your wife are able to pay your bills every month with a little left over? He and his wife have six-figure incomes and give large amounts of money to the church and other worthy causes.

Comparison takes God's good gifts and disparages them. Fueled by books, movies, and social media that paint unrealistic pictures of how life really is, comparison aches from unsatisfied hunger. Always yearning for something bigger, better, and shinier, a person who compares her spouse, her children, and her life with others' tears down her house with her own hands.

Busyness. Busyness is a sneaky foe. Disguising itself as productivity, busyness steals bricks from a home's foundation one by one. Too many extracurricular activities means eating dinner from paper bags en route to the next practice instead of sitting around the table talking and sharing life. An overabundance of volunteer tasks steals precious time from our primary callings as spouse, parent, and child.

As Oswald Chambers says, "The good is always the enemy of the best."[5] We cram our days so full of good things that we miss the best—time to study our Bibles and pray, time to attend church, time to sleep and relax. Busyness drains our energy to the point where all we have is leftovers for our spouse—scraps of attention and desire cobbled together at the end of the day. A too-busy person tears down her house with her own hands.

Disrespect. Disrespect can be subtle or in-your-face, but whatever approach it takes, it's dangerous. And contagious. And destructive. When we treat our spouses with disrespect, we reveal what's in our hearts—a sense of superiority, pride, and arrogance.

I'll never forgot the day my three-year-old spotted her daddy's shoes in the middle of the living room, put her hands on her hips, and said with scornful disdain, "Men! They never pick up after themselves."

Where did she learn these words? From me, of course. In an instant I realized that every time I spoke disrespectful, sarcastic, or critical words about my husband in my children's hearing, I tore him down before their eyes. Is it any wonder children rebel against and disrespect their parents when they become teenagers? Their parents have modeled this same behavior all their lives. A disrespectful person tears down her house with her own hands.

If you realize you've been tearing down your house in one or more of these ways, there's hope. As we consistently yield ourselves to

God, confess our sins daily, and invite Him to help us recognize and root out foolish thoughts and actions, we will become wise.

Instead of being a foolish person who destroys, we'll become a wise person who **builds**.

pleasure

I denied myself nothing my eyes desired;
I refused my heart no pleasure. My heart took delight
in all my labor, and this was the reward for all my toil.

Ecclesiastes 2:10

Some Old Testament readers suspect God is a cosmic killjoy. They often cite the book of Ecclesiastes to support their opinion and quote King Solomon's famous line:

"Vanity of vanities, all is vanity" (Ecclesiastes 1:2 NKJV).

Solomon set out "to study and to explore by wisdom all that is done under the heavens" (v. 13). In modern vernacular, he wanted to find the meaning of life.

Who better to embark on such a quest? Not only was he the wisest man on earth, he was also the richest. He had all the resources of the world at his disposal.

Like everything he tackled, Solomon threw himself into the pursuit wholeheartedly. He ate the most exquisite delicacies. He purchased the finest goods. Perhaps he thought accomplishment might bring meaning to his life, so he undertook building projects, created gardens, and designed elaborate structures.

"I amassed silver and gold for myself, and the treasure of kings and provinces. I acquired male and female singers, and a harem as well—the delights of a man's heart," he said (2:8).

Imagine that. Better yet, don't. Seven hundred wives and three hundred concubines. As harems go, his was (and still is) legendary.

At the end of it all, Solomon pronounced worldly pleasures meaningless. Nothing but God satisfies, he concluded. Temporary pleasure is just that—temporary.

So does this mean God frowns on entertainment, wealth, and physical pleasure? Not at all.

Sprinkled among Solomon's gloomy and cynical pronouncements about the emptiness of life, we find sparkling jewels of joy and happiness.

Take Ecclesiastes 2:24 for example: "A person can do nothing better than to eat and drink and find satisfaction in their own toil. This too, I see, is from the hand of God."

And Ecclesiastes 3:12: "I know that there is nothing better for people than to be happy and to do good while they live."

Scripture confirms what Solomon concludes, that God created the world and fills our lives with good things *for our good pleasure*. We find New Testament evidence of this in 1 Timothy 6:17: "Command those who are rich in this present world not to be arrogant nor to put their hope in wealth, which is so uncertain, but to put their hope in God, who richly provides us with *everything for our enjoyment*" (emphasis added).

God doesn't frown when His children find pleasure in the good things in life. He encourages it. Yet at the same time, He cautions, "Remember also your Creator" (Ecclesiastes 12:1 ESV), the giver of every good gift. Solomon's jaded perspective came about because he pursued wealth, accomplishments, and pleasure *apart from* God, not in partnership *with* God.

At the conclusion of his experiment, he tells his audience to remember they are created for more than this world. There's a far greater world to come—one that will make the finest palace seem like a garbage dump. God has prepared a kingdom that our words can't describe nor can our minds imagine.

Paul echoed Solomon when he said, "Command them to do good, to be rich in good deeds, and to be generous and willing to share. In this way they will lay up treasure for themselves as a firm foundation for the coming age, so that they may take hold of the life that is truly life" (1 Timothy 6:18–19).

It's not all about you, Paul said. The greatest pleasure is lasting pleasure—the one that lingers long after the meal is over, the money is spent, and the vacation ends.

That donation you made so a high school kid could go on a mission trip. That Compassion child you sponsored through adulthood. The thousand hours you volunteered in children's church. The endless meals you prepared for sick neighbors and grieving friends.

Pleasure that runs deep and fills our hearts with satisfaction doesn't come from crowding our lives with selfish pursuits. It comes when we enjoy God's blessings and share them with others—for His glory.

I heard a pastor say once, "When God blesses you, He doesn't even have you in mind." In this case, I disagree. He *does* have you in mind. He wants to bless you, and He wants to bless others through you. God's pockets go deep. When He lavishes His gifts of health, wisdom, energy, time, and money on you, He gives you enough to share with others.

He knows that when you invest in His kingdom by allowing His riches to flow through you, you'll experience life's greatest **pleasure**.

foxes

Catch for us the foxes, the little foxes that ruin the vineyards,
our vineyards that are in bloom.
Song of Songs 2:15

If you had to choose one word to focus on for a devotion about the Song of Songs, the racy book of the Bible that celebrates the joy of married sex, which would you choose? Would you focus on the physical perspective and choose *passion*? *Desire*? Or maybe *embrace*?

Or perhaps you'd take the more conservative approach. Even though Solomon, the author, never mentions God in this book, some scholars say it describes God's love for the church. If this is your perspective, you might choose a more reserved word, like *love*, or *commitment*, or *beloved*.

I chose the word *foxes*. Here's why.

In the midst of Solomon's romantic words to his bride-to-be—"Show me your face, let me hear your voice; for your voice is sweet, and your face is lovely" (Song of Songs 2:14)—he seems to go on a rabbit trail (or a fox trail?) when he inserts a warning about vermin in the vineyards.

"Catch for us the foxes, the little foxes that ruin the vineyards, our vineyards that are in bloom" (v. 15).

Is this squirrely moment totally random and completely disconnected from his passionate and flattering speech? I think not. Since 2 Timothy 3:16 tells us all Scripture is given by God and "useful for teaching, rebuking, correcting and training in righteousness," God had a good reason for including Solomon's aside in the poetic discourse of Song of Songs.

In Bible times, scavenging foxes prowled the countryside. They had the potential to destroy valuable vineyards such as the one where Solomon and his bride-to-be courted. In this case, however, Solomon isn't worried about grapes. He's protective of the growing romance.

Just as literal foxes can destroy physical property, figurative ones can harm relationships. Solomon says, in essence, "Let's do whatever it takes to protect our relationship from anything that can harm it."

What are these little foxes that can destroy any relationship?

Overcommitment is one of the most common. Long work hours, an overfull schedule, too many extracurriculars, and the inability to say no stretch us thinner than plastic wrap on a watermelon. We tag team kids, chores, and homework, seldom landing in the same place for more than a few hours. Absence in a relationship doesn't make the heart grow fonder. It makes it grow lonely.

Laziness is another little fox. When the excitement of a new relationship wanes and we settle into a routine, it's easy to put our efforts on cruise control. We kick back, put our metaphorical feet up, and take a pause. If we do expend energy, we do it in ways that benefit us instead of seeking ways to serve our spouse. We take each other for granted instead of actively and intentionally loving and serving.

A complaining spirit is a third little fox. The longer we're in a relationship, the better we know a person. Soon we see faults we never noticed (or chose to overlook). When someone fails to meet our (usually unrealistic) expectations, we grow disappointed. And cynical. And complaining. We nitpick everything, demand perfection, and voice our disapproval. Our relationship grows anemic as it bleeds from a thousand tiny wounds.

These three examples are only a sample of the little foxes that endanger marriages. Others include marital drift, discontentment, disillusionment, and boredom. The pack is large and prolific. If you examine your relationship carefully, you can spot the foxes threatening your vineyard. If you ignore them, they'll destroy your marriage.

Song of Songs celebrates the glorious institution of marriage. It smiles on the God-approved sexual intimacy of wedded bliss. But threaded through the narrative (three times, to be exact), Solomon inserted a God-inspired warning to the married among us—guard your marriage. And if you're not married, these same foxes can threaten friendships and other relationships.

Married or single, watch out for the little **foxes**.

rejoice

Behold, this is our God; we have waited for him,
that he might save us. This is the LORD; we have waited
for him; let us be glad and rejoice in his salvation.

Isaiah 25:9 ESV

Remember a time when you waited for something. Something you wanted badly. Something you knew would be the most wonderful thing in your life.

I waited for college graduation. This event, I was sure, would launch me into the glorious world of adulthood and autonomy. With that precious piece of paper in my hand, I could leave behind the limitations of youth and rise to take my place in the world.

Several months later, I waited for my wedding day. No longer would I be lonely and incomplete. My husband would supply everything that was missing in my life and devote himself to making me happy.

Five years after we said "I do," we waited for our first daughter to be born. The baby who stood on my bladder, pinched my sciatic nerve, and awakened me with her hiccups in the middle of the night would bring joy and happiness to our world.

Isaiah the prophet waited too. He waited for Israel to repent. He waited for the world to recognize the one true God. He waited for the Messiah to save His people from their sins. Most of all, he waited for God to usher in His forever kingdom.

The day I received my much-awaited college degree was a glorious one. My family gathered at a local restaurant and celebrated. That thin piece of parchment unlocked the door to my forty-year career as a dental hygienist. It also unlocked the door to long workdays, a stiff neck, and patients with cigarette breath.

And that marriage license? One hundred people gathered to witness our joy. It began almost forty years (so far) of learning to live with my best friend. It also began the challenge of trying to love each other well despite our tendencies to hurt and disappoint each other.

My nine-month wait for my precious daughter culminated in such overwhelming feelings of love I thought my heart would burst. David and I laughed, cried, and praised God for His goodness. Three days later colic began. Love covers a multitude of evils, but colic tested it to the limits.

Everything I've waited for and celebrated in this life has brought with it a mixture of joy and sorrow, triumph and trial.

But one day, Isaiah declares, Jesus will return, trials will disappear, and we will begin a celebration that will never end.

Someday, Isaiah wrote, Israel's eyes will be opened and they will embrace Jesus as their long-awaited Messiah. "I, the LORD, have called you in righteousness; I will take hold of your hand. I will keep you and will make you to be a covenant for the people and a light for the Gentiles, to open eyes that are blind, to free captives from prison and to release from the dungeon those who sit in darkness" (Isaiah 42:6–7).

God will usher in His kingdom with shouts of joy. "To me every knee shall bow, every tongue shall swear allegiance" (45:23 ESV).

The good news of salvation will spread on grateful tongues across all the world. "You will bring my salvation to the ends of the earth" (49:6 NLT).

And, finally, "He will swallow up death forever; and the Lord GOD will wipe away tears from all faces" (25:8 ESV).

It's not only okay but appropriate to celebrate the long-awaited things of this world. But are we also actively waiting for Jesus to come back? Do we live each day eager to celebrate His coming? Do we hold the things of this earth loosely, knowing a better world awaits us?

Be assured, something far superior is coming—something that will cause the things of this earth to grow strangely dim. No longer a mix of joy and sorrow, our forever lives will be more satisfying and marvelous than we can imagine.

Ponder this. Hold fast to the faith. Imagine what it will be like to celebrate with Isaiah, "Behold, this is our God; we have waited for him, that he might save us. This is the LORD; we have waited for him; let us be glad and rejoice in his salvation" (25:9 ESV).

No matter how long it takes for Jesus to return, wait. Be glad. **Rejoice**.

king

Who should not fear you, King of the nations?
This is your due. Among all the wise leaders of the nations
and in all their kingdoms, there is no one like you.

Jeremiah 10:7

What comes to mind when you picture a king? The stuff of fairy tales? Almost every movie I watched as a child featured a handsome prince with his doting father smiling indulgently from his throne. Rotund, clothed in velvet, and universally tame, movie kings were meant to be patted on the head, not feared or revered.

Even grown-up theater holds little respect for kings. Take, for example, the wildly popular Broadway musical *Hamilton*. In one of its most beloved numbers, England's King George III laments the breakup letter he's received from the American colonies with a pompous (but not very threatening) song called "You'll Be Back." Instead of cowering in fear at his plan to leverage the might of Britain to reclaim his wayward subjects, we chuckle at his arrogance.

Biblical history, however, paints a very different picture of a king. Powerful and sovereign, the kings in Bible days were feared and respected.

Yet even the most exalted earthly king pales in might and power before the greatest King of all, the King of Kings and Lord of Lords.

The prophet Jeremiah understood the might and majesty of God. "No one is like you, LORD," he wrote in Jeremiah 10:6–7. "You are great, and your name is mighty in power. Who should not fear you, King of the nations? This is your due. Among all the wise leaders of the nations and in all their kingdoms, there is no one like you."

Despite God's supremacy, the Israelites chafed at God's leadership. God had chosen to dwell among them and be their ruler, yet they rejected Him. Instead of bowing in humble submission to His perfectly wise and always best leadership, they stood in rebellion and declared their independence. "We want a king like all the other nations," they cried (see 1 Samuel 8:5).

Modern-day people follow in their rebellious footsteps. Instead of wanting to exchange our heavenly King for an earthly king, however, we prefer to have no king. We choose the rule of self-government, which is really no government at all. Like a two-year-old to her wise and loving father, we ball up our fists, plant our feet, and declare, "You're not the boss of me."

But God is.

As an artist owns his painting and a sculptor owns his statue, so God, our Master Designer, owns us. He formed us in the depths of our mothers' wombs and breathed life into our beings (Psalm 139:13). He alone has the right to govern our lives. He alone is worthy of worship.

David the psalmist acknowledged this when he penned Psalm 100, "Worship the LORD with gladness; come before him with joyful songs. Know that the LORD is God. It is he who made us, and we are his; we are his people, the sheep of his pasture" (vv. 1–3).

As the ruler over all creation, God rightfully commands the world and us in it. "God made the earth by his power," Jeremiah wrote. "He founded the world by his wisdom and stretched out the heavens by his understanding. When he thunders, the waters in the heavens roar; he makes clouds rise from the ends of the earth" (Jeremiah 10:12–13). As our Sovereign, He deserves our obedience. As our Savior, He deserves our love.

Jeremiah acknowledged God's right to guide his life. "Lord, I know that people's lives are not their own; it is not for them to direct their steps" (v. 23). In humble submission, he even trusted God to correct him when necessary, because he knew God sought only his best (v. 24).

We needn't fear or hesitate to pledge our allegiance to Him. Unlike wicked kings who abuse their power, God loves us with a perfect love. We can trust Him to order the events of our lives for our good. His ways aren't burdensome, because His ultimate goal is to draw us into a rich and full relationship with himself. He desires that we reach a place of obedience, fulfillment, and joy.

Hollywood and Broadway kings give us a glimmer of royalty, but one day we'll kneel before the one true King. We'll see Him in all His splendor and melt at His feet. When the breath returns to our lungs, we'll join our voices with Jeremiah and declare, "No one is like you, Lord; you are great, and your name is mighty in power. Who should not fear you, King of the nations? This is your due. Among all the wise leaders of the nations and in all their kingdoms, there is no one like you" (vv. 6–7).

Until that day, we can experience deep and abiding joy when we bow our hearts and surrender our lives to God Almighty, our wise and loving **King**.

cry

Even when I call out or cry for help, he shuts out my prayer.

Lamentations 3:8

Our family experienced a trial years ago greater than anything we'd ever walked through.

As is often the case, the day before the storm dawned bright and clear. Life hummed along quietly.

Until that phone call. That awful phone call.

Someone we loved was in crisis, and the outcome would impact us all. Fear and grief squeezed my heart. *Lord, I'm so afraid for him. And for us.*

The following morning, I stumbled out of bed, eyes almost swollen shut from the long night of crying.

I walked out of my bedroom and down the hall. Halfway there, muscle memory kicked in. I stepped into my study, settled into my chair, and reached for my journal and Bible. For years I'd begun my day talking with God in prayer and reading the Bible. Today I had nothing to bring to the conversation. I sat empty before the Lord.

I opened my journal and picked up a pen. Every morning I listed three things I was thankful for. That day I struggled to find even one.

Instead, I journaled my prayers. Great, gushing laments expressed the heartbreak of my soul. "Father, what are we to do," I wrote. "I'm grieving for him, and I'm grieving for our family. My heart is so sad."

Jeremiah the prophet understood the pain of lament. He, too, penned long, anguished prayers. The bleeding of his broken heart splashed onto the pages of Scripture:

"[God] has besieged me and surrounded me with bitterness and hardship. He has made me dwell in darkness like those long dead. He has walled me in so I cannot escape; he has weighed me down with chains. Even when I call out or cry for help, he shuts out my prayer" (Lamentations 3:5–8).

In the season of Jeremiah's distress, God seemed absent and uncaring. Or, worse yet, an enemy who tormented him with sorrow upon sorrow. Jeremiah knew, at any time, God could change the situation—but He didn't. Life as Jeremiah knew it would soon end, and an uncertain future loomed ahead.

When sinking in a quicksand of trial, instead of crying out to God, many shut Him out. They turn their backs on meeting with His people and spending time in His Word. "If this is how God treats those who serve Him," they say, "I want nothing to do with Him."

When the path grew difficult for Jesus's followers, many left. "'You do not want to leave too, do you?' Jesus asked the Twelve.

"Simon Peter answered him, 'Lord, to whom shall we go? You have the words of eternal life'" (John 6:67–68).

Jeremiah knew God was his only hope. Instead of allowing his grief to cut him off from his greatest source of comfort, he lamented before the Lord. He unleashed the geyser of his grief, and God met Him there.

"I called on your name, LORD, from the depths of the pit. You heard my plea: 'Do not close your ears to my cry for relief.' You came near when I called you, and you said, 'Do not fear'" (Lamentations 3:55–57).

I, too, reached out to God in my trial. I opened my Bible and found words of empathy and hope.

As I sat there, broken before Him, God wrapped His tender arms of love around me and spoke words of promise into my troubled soul. He spoke words of truth into my reeling mind. He spoke words of love into my sad heart. And He spoke words of courage into my trampled faith.

What comfort God's Word contains. God saw my tears and my sorrow. He understood my grief. He had not abandoned me. He felt closer than ever before.

God did this for Jeremiah too. He righted his toppled faith and restored his hope and perspective. The tender recipient of God's mercies, Jeremiah wrote:

"The LORD is good to those whose hope is in him, to the one who seeks him; it is good to wait quietly for the salvation of the LORD. . . . For no one is cast off by the Lord forever. Though he brings grief, he will show compassion, so great is his unfailing love. For he does not willingly bring affliction or grief to anyone" (vv. 25–26, 31–33).

Jeremiah and I learned that God's children don't have to put on a brave face when we approach Him. We can come to Him in our grief, and He will meet us there.

God hears us when we **cry**.

know

Then you will know that I am the LORD.

Ezekiel 20:42

Trials often blindside us. Although some creep into our lives, others leap out of dark alleys and clobber us. One moment we're strolling along happily, and the next—*wham!*—we're lying on the pavement wondering what just happened.

Sometimes this happens literally, like the friend who stepped out onto her deck to water the plants and found herself at the foot of the stairs with a broken hip. Other times trials come in the form of a job loss, family crisis, or sudden death. With no time to prepare, we're left reeling, swaying from one emotion to the next. Fear, grief, and confusion pummel us until we're emotionally and spiritually battered.

In times like these, God's sovereignty can be a mighty comfort. But we can also stumble over it.

I often struggle with God's sovereign control when tragedy or trial enters my life. Knowing God could prevent bad things from happening, I wonder why He allows them.

The Old Testament book of Ezekiel cracks the curtain on the *why* behind the *what* of trials. Sixty-seven times God used the same phrase to explain His purpose in allowing abundance and scarcity, triumphs and trials, judgment and mercy to come upon the world.

"Then you will know that I am the Lord" (Ezekiel 20:42).

Although I don't like to think about it sometimes, God has more in mind for my life than my comfort. His plan is grander, higher, and better than pain-free, trial-less lives for us all. The ultimate purpose of mankind, as the Westminster Catechism declares, "is to glorify God, and to enjoy him for ever."[6]

The more I study Scripture, the more I realize God has three basic purposes for everything that happens in this world.

First, He seeks to reconcile all to himself who would believe. He often uses the trials of this life to help us realize how much we need a relationship with Him. Many a soul has cried out to God for salvation when they reach the end of themselves. When they discover they need someone wiser and stronger than they are to direct their lives.

We see this first purpose when God declared to Ezekiel why He judged the godless nation of Egypt.

"When I make Egypt desolate and strip the land of everything in it, when I strike down all who live there, then they will know that I am the Lord" (32:15).

But what if we already have a relationship with God? What if we've surrendered our lives to His control? Why do we sometimes suffer hardship?

The second and third purposes for suffering are that it refines and matures our faith, and it provides a way to glorify God before others.

Blessings seldom grow our faith. They're the ice cream in our spiritual diet—an unexpected treat. Trials are the meat and veggies that make us strong. God uses scary times to prove that He can and will take care of us. He uses correction to direct us away from harmful paths. He uses heartbreak to help us learn that when all is stripped away, God remains—and He is enough.

When our lives are trouble free, it's easy for our spiritual muscles to grow flabby. We often become entitled, ungrateful, and demanding. We toss God an occasional crumb of gratitude, but don't feel the need to spend regular time with Him. Avoiding deeper times of Bible study and prayer, we dabble at the edges.

We remain spiritual babies content to crawl when God wants us to run.

Paul recorded God's purpose in allowing hardship in the lives of His chosen people. "Not only that, but we rejoice in our sufferings, knowing that suffering produces endurance, and endurance produces character, and character produces hope" (Romans 5:3–4). God also uses blessings and trials to showcase His glory.

We love the blessing part. It's easy to talk about God when He opens up the windows of heaven and drenches us with His goodness. But in the upside-down economy of God, trials usually carry more value in the bank of eternity.

Didn't Satan say to God, "Does Job fear God for nothing? . . . Have you not put a hedge around him and his household and everything he has? You have blessed the work of his hands, so that his flocks and herds are spread throughout the land. But now stretch out your hand and strike everything he has, and he will surely curse you to your face" (Job 1:9–11).

Don't misunderstand. God doesn't roam throughout the earth scattering affliction like some sadistic, power-hungry egomaniac. But when the difficulties of living in a sin-sick world touch our lives, He uses them to showcase His power and point people to himself. When others see how God sustains His children despite grievous hardships, they take notice.

The world knows, as Job's wife suggested, that we can curse God and die. Or we can declare our trust in Him no matter what. When a Christian stands in faith instead of crumbling in fear, God gets the glory and people are drawn to Him. Genuine faith is winsome and beautiful. When we suffer in faith, we accurately represent Christ to a world desperately searching for something (or Someone) to believe in.

"And so I will show my greatness and my holiness," God said in Ezekiel 38:23, "and I will make myself known in the sight of many nations. Then they will know that I am the LORD."

Because we live in a fallen world, sickness, heartache, and difficulty come upon us all. But rest assured, God never wastes our pain.

In His mission to draw unbelievers to himself, He orchestrates every event of their lives. Is that prodigal you're praying for enjoying success? Perhaps God is extending His goodness to lead them to repentance (Romans 2:4). Are they suffering under trials and hardship? God may be allowing affliction to draw them to himself (Psalm 119:71).

For believers, He allows blessings and hardships to make us more like Jesus and point others to himself.

Believer or unbeliever, blessing or trial, we can rest in the certainty that God has one overarching purpose for everything that comes into our lives:

"That you will **know**."

if

If we are thrown into the blazing furnace, the God we serve
is able to deliver us from it, and he will deliver us from
Your Majesty's hand. But even if he does not,
we want you to know, Your Majesty, that we will not serve
your gods or worship the image of gold you have set up.

Daniel 3:17–18

All my life I've been stalked by an army of ifs.

When I was a child, the if army looked a lot like the bogeyman. *If a witch comes out of the attic, she'll eat you while you sleep. If your mom forgets to lock the door, a troll might sneak in and carry you away.*

In high school, when I had to make grown-up decisions that would impact my life for decades, the ifs seemed more like a sniper corps. *If you don't score high enough on the SAT, you won't get into college. If you don't choose the right profession, you'll be stuck forever in a job you hate.*

When I married, had children, and grew wiser to the ebb and flow of life, the ifs became a full battalion and gained more ammunition with which to frighten me. *If your husband gets killed in a car wreck, you'll be left to raise the girls by yourself. If your kids hang out with the wrong crowd, they'll turn their backs on their faith. If the wrong people get elected to office, our country will be destroyed.*

At first, I tried psychology and positive mantras to fend off the attacks. I told myself that most of what we worry about never comes true. But then I'd hear stories about a godly friend whose husband cheated on her or a neighbor whose child was killed by a drunk driver. My "that couldn't happen to you" defense disappeared faster than an F-15.

Bad things happen. Consider Shadrach, Meshach, and Abednego. Busted for not bowing down to the king's idolatrous statue, these three Israelites found themselves squarely in the sights of an if sniper.

"Now when you hear the sound of the horn, flute, zither, lyre, harp, pipe and all kinds of music, if you are ready to fall down and worship the image I made, very good. But if you do not worship it, you will be thrown immediately into a blazing furnace. Then what god will be able to rescue you from my hand?" (Daniel 3:15).

Psychology and positive thoughts weren't going to deliver these three. To ignore or pretend the threat wasn't real weren't options either. As they stood in the crosshairs of death, they had two choices—deny the God they served and avoid the fire or stand in faith and burn.

The three young men squared their shoulders, looked the if in the eye, and staked their faith claim.

"If we are thrown into the blazing furnace, the God we serve is able to deliver us from it, and he will deliver us from Your Majesty's hand.

"But even if he does not, we want you to know, Your Majesty, that we will not serve your gods or worship the image of gold you have set up" (vv. 17–18).

Facts are facts, and Scripture backs them up. Jesus said, "In this world you will have trouble" (John 16:33). It is true. Bad things happen. Faith is not a cloaking device to render us invisible to trials.

Shadrach, Meshach, and Abednego faced the army of ifs, and God was with them. He was their defense. He's our defense too.

When ifs threaten us, instead of cowering, turning away, or pretending they don't exist, we can haul them out before the firing squad and watch them quake.

If God chooses not to deliver us, and we're thrown into the fiery furnace, He will go with us. He'll use our trials to showcase His presence and display His glory to the watching world.

If I get cancer, God will walk with me every step of the way and not waste a moment of my pain.

If my husband leaves me, God will be my protector, provider, and advocate.

If my child turns her back on God and walks away, God will pursue her down every dark alley and use every heartbreaking circumstance in her life to draw her back.

If I suffer financial loss, grief, or pain, God will meet my needs according to His riches in glory.

What army of ifs is stalking you today? Grab it by the throat. Hold it up to the God who loved you enough to die for you. Determine to walk in faith—even **if**.

door

Therefore I am now going to allure her; I will lead her into the
wilderness and speak tenderly to her. There I will give her back her
vineyards, and will make the Valley of Achor a door of hope.

Hosea 2:14–15

Melissa never intended to steal another woman's husband. Recently
divorced and struggling to heal, the last thing she wanted was a
relationship.

Her coworker Jason was handsome. Kind. Thoughtful. And
married.

On staff at a megachurch in Atlanta, they worked together on
different ministry projects. He led the youth group. She handled the
church's IT needs. During planning meetings, she noticed his heart
for God. He noticed her gentle spirit.

He held the door for her one night after the weekly meeting and
walked with her to the parking lot.

"You shared some great ideas in the meeting tonight," he said. "I
can't wait to see what God does through this."

"I love my job," she responded. "And I really appreciate your leadership. I can tell you care about the students and want to see them grow in the Lord." They climbed into their respective cars and went home—Melissa to her two children and Jason to his wife.

The next week after the planning meeting, he was again at the door with a kind smile and words of appreciation. This time they lingered under the streetlight, swapping ideas for a new YouTube channel. Conversation drifted into personal waters and an hour passed before they noticed the time and parted ways.

You know the rest of the story. This same scenario, with different characters and in different settings, plays itself out every day. Relationships that begin innocently get sucked into the riptide of emotional and physical adultery that drowns marriages, families, and ministries.

When the passion and excitement of Melissa and Jason's romance cooled, the weight of their sin crashed down upon them. Their sin stood like a wall between them and God.

Their spirits ached. Their prayers fell flat. They bled from a thousand places where the Holy Spirit had pierced their souls. They knew they'd have no rest until they made things right with God and those they had sinned against.

The nations of Israel and Judah suffered a similar fate. They had turned their backs on God to chase after other lovers. Forsaking the One who had led them through the wilderness, fed them manna from heaven, protected them from mighty armies, and loved them as His own, they committed spiritual adultery with the false gods of the surrounding nations.

In love, God afflicted them. The prophet Hosea described why God often withdraws His blessings:

> For I will be like a lion to Ephraim, like a great lion
> to Judah. I will tear them to pieces and go away; I will
> carry them off, with no one to rescue them. Then I

will return to my lair *until they have borne their guilt and seek my face—in their misery they will earnestly seek me.* (Hosea 5:14–15; emphasis added)

Tasked with pointing the wayward Israelites back to God, Hosea made this plea:

> Come, let us return to the Lord. He has torn us to pieces but he will heal us; he has injured us but he will bind up our wounds. (6:1)

In His willingness to draw His children back to himself, God provides what Hosea 2:15 calls "a door of hope."

When His wayward ones walk through this door, when they accept His invitation to leave their faithless ways and return to Him with all their hearts, God makes a promise:

"I will betroth you to me forever; I will betroth you in righteousness and justice, in love and compassion. I will betroth you in faithfulness, and you will acknowledge the LORD" (2:19–20).

A biblical counselor reminded Melissa and Jason of God's forgiving heart and pointed them to the door of hope. They couldn't undo the damage their sin had done to Jason's marriage, their testimonies, and their spiritual lives, but they could seek God's forgiveness and start over.

I pray none of us ever gets sucked into the tangled web of adultery or any other form of habitual sin, but if we do, God provides a path to restoration.

"Sow righteousness for yourselves," Hosea instructed. "Reap the fruit of unfailing love, and break up your unplowed ground; for it is time to seek the LORD, until he comes and showers his righteousness on you" (10:12).

Are you caught in a sin you never imagined you'd be involved in? Do you know someone who is? God has made a way for His wayward children to return—a path to forgiveness, healing, and restoration. Accept the hope He offers and escape from the valley of sin. Walk through the **door**.

rains

Be glad, people of Zion, rejoice in the LORD your God, for he has given you the autumn rains because he is faithful. He sends you abundant showers, both autumn and spring rains, as before.

Joel 2:23

When you're in a desert, you fear you'll never see rain again.

I felt this way as our mission team traveled between Cabo San Lucas and La Paz, Mexico. Crammed into an ancient nine-passenger Suburban with eight sweaty students and three miserable chaperones, I felt like a chicken in an air fryer.

The temperature outside hovered around one hundred degrees. The temperature inside wasn't much cooler. The intermittent air conditioner coughed out bursts of cold air followed by wheezes of heat. Every so often water would sputter from the vent in the dash, dribbling onto the teenager straddling the console. She quit complaining when she realized the water running down her leg was the coolest thing in the SUV.

Blindly following our mission team leader in the car ahead, we drove on empty dirt roads through cactus forests. Dust filtered through the vents, covering us with orange grit. Halfway there, a bridge rose up out of nowhere, spanning a dry riverbed dotted with rocks.

"When the rains come," our guide told us, "the rivers flood and the roads become impassable. But 355 days a year, it's dry."

This was my first experience with a desert, but the Israelites knew it well. Unlike the fertile lowlands of neighboring Egypt watered by the Nile, Israel had no permanent source of water. Its land sat high on a peninsula far above the rivers. Moses described it in Deuteronomy 11:10–11:

> The land you are entering to take over is not like the land of Egypt, from which you have come, where you planted your seed and irrigated it by foot as in a vegetable garden. But the land you are crossing the Jordan to take possession of is a land of mountains and valleys that drinks rain from heaven.

When He settled His people in the land, God made a promise: "If you faithfully obey the commands I am giving you today—to love the LORD your God and to serve him with all your heart and with all your soul—then I will send rain on your land in its season, both autumn and spring rains, so that you may gather in your grain, new wine and olive oil" (Deuteronomy 11:13–14). If you don't, He warned, I "will shut up the heavens so that it will not rain and the ground will yield no produce" (v. 17).

Fast forward several hundred years to the dark days of apostasy. Joel writes about them in the three-chapter book that bears his name. The nation had turned its collective back on God, committing spiritual adultery and refusing to walk in His ways.

To draw them back, God allowed horrible circumstances to come upon them: plagues of locusts, hordes of invading armies, and a deep and persistent drought. As He had promised, He shut up the heavens. The crops failed. Pasture lands dried up. Man and beast began to starve.

God's people were in the desert—physically *and* spiritually.

Sometimes we find ourselves in the desert too. Perhaps, like the Israelites, sin has forced us into a barren place. Other times someone else's choices—an unbelieving husband or a wayward child—bring us there. Circumstances beyond our control, like a chronic health condition, a broken marriage, or the death of a dream flings us out into the cactus forest and leaves us dusty, battered, and dry.

Regardless of whether we're trudging through the desert of sin, circumstances, or sorrow, God offers hope. Listen to His words to the Israelites (and to us): "'Even now,' declares the LORD, 'return to me with all your heart, with fasting and weeping and mourning'" (Joel 2:12).

The prophet Joel gave further instructions. "Rend your heart and not your garments. Return to the LORD your God, for he is gracious and compassionate, slow to anger and abounding in love, and he relents from sending calamity" (v. 13).

Joel directed his words to faithless Israel, but they apply to us as well. Whether we're languishing in the desert because of our own sin, someone else's, or the hot winds of circumstance, we can throw ourselves at God's feet and beg for His mercy. When we turn to Him "with all [our] heart, with fasting and weeping and mourning" (v. 12), God will refresh us with a downpour of His grace and mercy.

To the repentant sinner, He extends the cleansing rain of forgiveness. To the battered believer, He sends showers of comfort and strength. The former rains prove God will send more rain.

Remember those years when He provided, protected, and interceded for you? He'll do it again. The seasons when He held you close and comforted you when you cried? His compassionate arms never grow weary. His character does not change. His love is lavish.

"Be glad, people of Zion, rejoice in the LORD your God, for he has given you the autumn rains because he is faithful. He sends you abundant showers, both autumn and spring rains, as before" (v. 23).

Although the cloudless sky stretched blue and clear in every direction, the prophet Joel reminded the Israelites (and us today), that relief was on the horizon.

Turn to Him in your trial. Repent if necessary. Weep. Fast and seek His face. Watch for your faithful God to move. At the right time, He will send the **rains**.

famine

"The days are coming," declares the Sovereign LORD, "when I will send a famine through the land—not a famine of food or a thirst for water, but a famine of hearing the words of the LORD."

Amos 8:11

For years I seldom opened my Bible. Like my favorite purse, I carried it to church on Sundays and Wednesday nights. When the pastor introduced the text of his sermon, I'd flip to the passage and follow along. If I attended a Bible study, I'd look up verses in my Bible and pencil in my answers on the worksheet. My Bible was a tool, not a treasure.

Then I read the online article from the *Christian Post*, "Chinese Christians Memorize Bible in Prison: Gov't 'Can't Take What's Hidden in Your Heart.'"[7] The piece shared the stories of believers who memorize huge portions and even entire books of the Bible. At a seminar, eighteen of the twenty-two Christians attending had been imprisoned for their faith. One woman shared how in prison "you have much time." She spent it memorizing Scripture.

Although guards confiscate Bibles and other Christian material, believers smuggle in portions of the Word of God on scraps of paper. "We memorize it as fast as we can," the woman said, "because even though they can take the paper away, they can't take what's hidden in your heart."

Amos prophesied about a famine of the Word of God. He may have been talking about a day to come where the physical Word of God, the Bible, is banned. Or he could have in mind a time when Christian influence and the preaching and teaching of God's Word is scarce.

> "The days are coming," declares the Sovereign LORD, "when I will send a famine through the land—not a famine of food or a thirst for water, but a famine of hearing the words of the LORD. People will stagger from sea to sea and wander from north to east, searching for the word of the LORD, but they will not find it." (Amos 8:11–12)

The Chinese Christians' love for and commitment to God's Word motivates me. The scarcity of Bibles in their world makes even one verse of Scripture a precious treasure. Every encounter they have with the Bible is a feast and a delight.

Compared with my brothers and sisters in China, I'm a Bible glutton. My home holds enough contraband that if I lived in their country, I'd be imprisoned for life. Or executed.

A quick scan of my bookshelves unearthed more than twenty Bibles: three copies of the *John MacArthur Daily Bible* I use every morning; three copies of *The Chronological Bible*; the cardboard-cover *Holy Bible* I received at vacation Bible school; the *Scofield Reference Bible* I received at my baptism; my late mother-in-law's Bible; my late brother-in-law's Bible; the Bible I bought to give to my granddaughter on her birthday; and so on, and so on, and so on.

I've come a long way in the thirty-five years since I carried my Bible as an accessory. Now I read my Bible almost every day. But it's been too long since I memorized a passage of Scripture. The days are coming—and in some places are already here—when there will be a famine of the Word of God.

What would happen if the authorities declared it illegal to gather for worship and prayer? Would our lives be any different, or do we treat our commitment to God's people so lightly that a government decree would barely impact our lives? Would we know God's Word well enough to feed ourselves and our family from its pages?

If all twenty of my Bibles were taken away tomorrow, would I have enough spiritual food in my mental refrigerator to stay alive? To thrive? To share with others?

I suspect not.

It's time to remedy this. First Corinthians 4:2 says, "Now it is required that those who have been given a trust must prove faithful." We have been entrusted with the amazing privileges of being able to own a Bible and freely meet for worship and study, and we must faithfully steward the gifts God has given us.

The brave, dedicated, courageous Chinese Christians have taught me that believers everywhere must prepare now for the days of spiritual leanness. A day is coming, Amos warns, when access to the preaching and teaching of God's Word (and perhaps the Bible itself) will be limited. We must treasure and learn from God's Word now so we can weather the day of **famine**.

pride

The pride of your heart has deceived you, you who live in the
clefts of the rocks and make your home on the heights, you who
say to yourself, "Who can bring me down to the ground?"

Obadiah 1:3

With rare exception, pride is ugly, off-putting, and distasteful. God
hates it (Proverbs 8:13).

But what is pride? One dictionary defines it as "a high or inordi-
nate opinion of one's own dignity, importance, merit, or superiority,
whether as cherished in the mind or as displayed in bearing, conduct, etc."[8]

The Bible bursts with examples of pride with skin on. The book
of Esther describes evil Haman, an arrogant man waxing eloquently
about his accomplishments. He was so in love with himself that he
invited his friends and family to his home to listen to him brag about
all he had done (Esther 5:10–11). I suspect if we checked his birth
certificate, we'd see *Pride* listed as his middle name.

Isaiah wrote about a charismatic leader with big visions who per-suaded multitudes to blindly follow him. Sound familiar? Satan was so filled with pride he led a revolution in heaven to dethrone God (Isaiah 14:12–14).

What about an atheist who thumbs his nose at God and declares, "I am the center of my universe"? Yep, he's in there too. David, the writer of Psalm 14, called him by his common name: *fool* (v. 1).

The prophet Obadiah wrote to the arrogant nation of Edom and delivered a pronouncement from God: "The pride of your heart has deceived you" (Obadiah v. 3).

Edom's pride was easy to spot. The country boasted in its military prowess, gloated over its armies, and flaunted its wickedness. If ever a country was deceived by its pride, it was Edom.

But what about us? Are sincere Christians who are doing our best to live for God immune to pride? Although showy displays of self-glorification certainly characterize pride, it often wears other faces. Subtle faces. Faces that look a lot like mine . . . and yours.

These other faces of pride say:

"I'm right." I'm not talking about the absolutes of Scripture, but the opinions and preferences we all hold. This type of pride often manifests itself in relationships. Husbands and wives struggle for power within their marriages. Church members push their views and agendas without listening to the thoughts of others. Friends fall out over matters of preference or perspective. Whenever we exalt our subjective opinion above others', we fall victim to pride.

"I don't need help. I can do it myself." If you've been around a toddler for any length of time, you've heard these two sentences spo-ken forcefully. Usually we celebrate them (although they aggravate the daylights out of us), because they demonstrate a child's growing independence. When we hear these words coming from an adult's mouth, however, they often reveal a prideful heart.

The person who says this prefers to be the one who gives help instead of receiving it. We like to demonstrate our competency and strength, not any sign of weakness or helplessness. We'd rather suffer loss than admit we can't do it all. This, my friend, is pride.

"You are amazing. I could never serve God as well." While these words masquerade as a cloak of humility, they cover up a prideful heart. One that looks inward, not upward. Instead of embracing the unique and valuable gifts God has given us, we compare ours with others'. *She's such a good speaker. He's so wise. She is talented and beautiful, and I'm not.*

Self-denigration is one of the easiest pride traps to fall into. When we stumble into it, our actions say, "God, you made me wrong. If I were God, I would have given me the gifts and abilities I need. I would have done better than you." When we embrace the truth that God has given us "everything we need for a godly life" (2 Peter 1:3), we can walk in confidence and faith, not envy and fear.

The tiny book of Obadiah reminds us pride is dangerously deceptive. It sets us at odds with God and stands in the way of His grace. "God opposes the proud," James 4:6 says, "but shows favor to the humble."

I don't know about you, but I don't want God to oppose me. I need His help every moment. When we listen to others' opinions, accept help when necessary, and embrace the gifts and abilities He's given us, we humble ourselves before Him. When we do, God promises to lift us up (v. 10).

Whenever God exalts anyone, it's by His grace alone. There's no room for **pride**.

provided

Now the LORD provided a huge fish to swallow Jonah, and Jonah
was in the belly of the fish three days and three nights.

Jonah 1:17

If you were on a television game show and had to answer the question, "What is the name of a famous children's Bible story?" what would you say? Many of us might respond, "Jonah and the whale."

And if we had to summarize the story to win the bonus question? My six-year-old granddaughter, Caroline, could win that prize.

She showed me her Sunday school coloring page and announced, "We learned about Jonah and the whale today."

"What did you learn about Jonah?"

She thought a moment, studied the picture of the seaweed-covered prophet staggering out of the sea as the fish bobbed on the waves behind him, and said, "If we disobey God, baaaaad things happen."

We nodded, mutually wide-eyed at the thought of being swallowed by a whale, spending three days and nights in a fish's belly, and then being burped out onto the shore.

"Bet that fish had an awful tummy ache," she said, and our serious conversation dissolved into giggles.

Caroline was right to recognize obedience as the theme of the book of Jonah, but I'd like to spotlight a word you might not have noticed: *provided*. "Now the LORD provided a huge fish to swallow Jonah, and Jonah was in the belly of the fish three days and three nights" (Jonah 1:17).

For years I pictured the sailors tossing Jonah into the stormy seas to appease his angry God. In a classic example of going from bad to worse, as Jonah sinks into the sea, a giant fish happens along, and eats him for lunch. Talk about poor timing.

Yet *provided* is a very intentional word. I provide food for my family. I provide dental advice for my patients. I provide transportation for my parents. When we provide for someone, we deliberately supply what they need.

What did Jonah need?

To repent and do what God had called him to do.

God's command to Jonah was clear: "Go to the great city of Nineveh and preach against it, because its wickedness has come up before me" (v. 2). Jonah did the opposite: "But Jonah ran away from the LORD and headed for Tarshish. He went down to Joppa, where he found a ship bound for that port. After paying the fare, he went aboard and sailed for Tarshish to flee from the LORD" (v. 3).

Thankfully, God didn't abandon Jonah in his rebellion. He sent a storm. Then He appointed a great fish to rescue Jonah from drowning and sustain him for three days and nights.

Imagine floating in gastric juices surrounded by partially digested fish and seaweed for seventy-two hours. One hour would have done it for me, but Jonah was stubborn. When he finally came to his senses, he surrendered to God's will and repented of his disobedience.

Truth be told, we're not much different from Jonah. Most of us aren't running from a call to missions (although some might), but we struggle to obey God every day. Do we obey His call to purity in the media we consume (Psalm 101:3)? Do we submit to His command to be an active member of a local church (Hebrews 10:25)? Do we conduct ourselves with honesty and integrity in our workplaces (Leviticus 19:11)?

When we don't, what does God provide for us?

The same thing He provided for Jonah—a way back. A path to repentance and obedience.

Sometimes, as with Jonah, God provides consequences—natural results or divine judgment—for our sinful actions. More often than we deserve, God leads us to repentance through His goodness (Romans 2:4), but if we're particularly stubborn, God will discipline us (Proverbs 3:11).

Even this is mercy. As a loving father seeks to train his children, so God, our heavenly Father, trains us to walk in "paths of righteousness for his name's sake" (Psalm 23:3 ESV).

God also provides forgiveness. If we humble ourselves, confess our sin, and seek to obey Him, He promises to forgive us. Every time (1 John 1:9).

God provided Jesus to make a way for sinful people to receive forgiveness of their sins and experience a relationship with God (John 3:16).

God provides the Holy Spirit to prick our hearts when we sin (John 16:7–8 NLT). Like the red light flashing on our dashboard, Holy Spirit conviction warns us. If we don't remove sin from our lives, we'll damage our relationship with God, ourselves, and others.

Finally, once we've repented, God provides the strength we need to do the good works He calls us to do (Hebrews 13:21). Even when it's hard. Especially when it's hard.

After Jonah surrendered to God's call, God enabled him to preach salvation to one of the wickedest nations on earth. He can empower us to love that difficult family member. Remain faithful to our marriage vows. Care for that parent, child, or spouse. Resist that temptation.

I'm so grateful God doesn't allow us to wander (or walk) away from Him. If we've truly surrendered our lives to Him, as the prophet Jonah did, God promises to walk with us all the days of our lives. He who began a good work in us will be faithful to complete it (Philippians 1:6).

Whether God's work in us involves blessing, correction, or judgment, we can trust His motives and His methods. He who loved us enough to die for us (Romans 8:32) has already appointed the events of our lives for our good and His glory. We can trust what He's **provided**.

pardons

Where is another God like you, who pardons the guilt
of the remnant, overlooking the sins of his special people?

Micah 7:18 NLT

If you're like me, you try very hard to forget your sins.

When I do, they fall into two categories: BC sins and AC sins. The BC sins are those I committed before Christ came into my life. This is a very long list. I had eighteen years to build it.

My list includes—among others I'd care not to mention—selfishness, dishonesty, and cruel words, deeds, and thoughts. I lived for myself and whatever I thought would make me happy, regardless of the pain it caused others.

Most people called me a "good" kid because I studied hard, stayed away from the wrong crowd, and chose not to smoke, drink, or use drugs. But I knew the truth—my life was all about me.

Even the good I did for others was self-serving. I obeyed my parents (for the most part) not to bring them joy or honor them, but so it would go well for me. I didn't break the law, not because I desired to live uprightly, but because I didn't want to be punished. I attended church not because I desired to know God better, but because my friends were there. Romans 14:23 says, "Everything that does not come from faith is sin," so I was a sinner.

Then there are the AC sins—the sins I committed (and continue to commit) after I placed my faith in Christ. I've had more than thirty years to collect these, so their number is also considerable.

At first glance, this list isn't as blatantly offensive as the first. It contains fewer "big uglies" and more "small slimmies"—the sins that are easy to hide behind a fake smile and a well-timed "Bless your heart." Pride, unforgiveness, selfishness, and self-righteousness top this list.

It's funny, but at night when sleep evades me and my mind scrolls back through my life, I find it easier to accept God's forgiveness for my BC sins than for my AC sins. My BC sins don't torment me as much, because, without the Spirit of God in my life, I had no hope of behaving in ways that pleased God. I sinned because I was a sinner.

But then there are my AC sins—the sins I committed after the Spirit of God came to live inside me. I find it harder to accept forgiveness for these sins, because I should have known better. Somehow I expected my life (and my behavior) to transform immediately after accepting Christ as my Savior, but it didn't. I still sin.

I should have yielded to the Holy Spirit when He whispered, *Don't do that.* I should have obeyed the Bible verse that warned me not to covet someone's success, steal time from my employer, or lie to avoid a reprimand.

Before Christ, I sinned because I was a sinner. After Christ, I sin because I choose to. How can I accept God's forgiveness for this type of willful disobedience? "What kind of Christian are you?" Satan whispers in those dark moments when no one is around. "Jesus lives in your heart, and you still behave this way?"

It is in these moments that the words of Micah the prophet speak truth and banish Satan's lies:

"Where is another God like you, who pardons the guilt of the remnant, overlooking the sins of his special people? You will again have compassion on us; you will tread our sins underfoot and hurl all our iniquities into the depths of the sea" (Micah 7:18–19).

The word *pardons* sparkles like a gem in this passage. It's a legal term that means to use the executive power of a leader to forgive a person convicted of a crime. This action removes any penalties or punishments related to the crime and prevents new prosecution.

When I was eighteen years old, I confessed my sin to God and asked Him to forgive me. This is when God pardoned me. He not only forgave me, He removed the penalty for my sins. He symbolically stamped my account with the word that Jesus shouted from the cross, *tetelestai*, "It is finished" (John 19:30). The debt has been paid in full.

Unlike me, God sees no difference between my BC sins and my AC sins. Christ paid the penalty for them all—past, present, and future. It is on this basis that I am forgiven. But that's not all. After He forgave me, He cast my sin (all of it) into the depths of the sea to remember it no more (Micah 7:19).

"I know God has forgiven me," people sometimes say, "but I can't forgive myself." On the surface this sounds pious and repentant, but in reality this type of reasoning elevates our feelings above God's actions. To hold on to guilt after God has declared us clean diminishes Christ's work on the cross and makes it impossible for us to walk in freedom.

If you, like me, try hard not to think about your sins, perhaps we should try a different approach. Instead of shamefully looking the other way or allowing guilt to hamstring us, let's look our sins squarely in the eye and remember that they have been forgiven and forgotten. Only then can we walk in the freedom that comes when God **pardons**.

but

The LORD is good, a refuge in times of trouble. He cares for those
who trust in him, but with an overwhelming flood he will make an
end of Nineveh; he will pursue his foes into the realm of darkness.

Nahum 1:7–8

I've never been so humiliated in my life.

My children and I were wrapping up a study of the judicial system
in homeschool one year. I discovered that the county courthouse allowed student tours when the court wasn't in session.

"If you're lucky," the clerk of court said when I called to make
arrangements, "Judge Gardner might be in his chambers. If he is, he
might come out and speak with the students."

On the day of the tour, our group waited outside the courthouse
while I stepped in to tell the clerk we'd arrived. After I introduced
myself, a man with tortoiseshell glasses and kind eyes stepped up
and extended his hand.

"I'm Judge Gardner," he said with a smile. "I'm glad you're here.
I love having homeschool groups tour the courtroom. The students

always ask great questions." We exchanged pleasantries, then he excused himself to don his robes.

We filed into the courtroom, and the clerk of court briefed us on courtroom etiquette.

"This is a court of law," she said sternly. "There will be no talking. You will rise when the judge enters the chambers and sit when instructed. You will only speak when called upon and only if given permission by the judge. If you have a question, raise your hand, and wait until the judge acknowledges you. Then stand to address the bench. Are there any questions?"

Silence reigned in the courtroom. The students exchanged wide-eyed glances and squirmed. One of the younger children let out a nervous giggle. A frown from the clerk silenced the offender.

"All rise. The Honorable Judge Gardner presiding," she said. We shot to our feet like basic training recruits in the presence of a drill sergeant.

For the next ten minutes the judge shared the history of the court, the courthouse, and his role as Circuit Court justice.

"Now, enough from me," he said. "I'd like to hear from you. Who has a question?"

The students, in awe of the judge and still slightly terrified of the clerk of court, sat silent and still. Thinking I'd break the ice by asking the first question, I raised my hand.

"Yes, ma'am," the judge said, acknowledging me.

"The brochure said . . ." I began, only to be interrupted by the judge's booming voice.

"YOU WILL STAND WHEN YOU ADDRESS THE COURT."

I jumped to my feet, legs wobbling and knees shaking. My heart constricted, and a red flush spread from my chest to my hairline. All eyes were upon me, the group leader who had broken protocol and offended the court.

I stammered out my question about the jury box and managed to remain standing until the judge turned his eyes on someone else. Shame and mortification lingered over me for the rest of the field trip. Later, after we'd toured the building and prepared to exit, Judge Gardner pulled me aside.

"Mrs. Hatcher, I'm sorry for making an example out of you," he said. "It's very important the students know that a court of law is a serious place. A place with rules and protocol. I don't ever want them to treat the judicial system and its public servants lightly. If they learn to respect the system now, it may spare them a lot of heartache in the future."

That day I saw the two faces of Judge Gardner. The kind gentleman and the righteous judge. The prophet Nahum would have felt right at home with Judge Gardner.

In the first chapter of the book that bears his name, Nahum the prophet displays the stunning contrast between the two faces of God, our strong refuge and ultimate judge.

"The LORD is good, a refuge in times of trouble. He cares for those who trust in him, *but* with an overwhelming flood he will make an end of Nineveh; he will pursue his foes into the realm of darkness" (Nahum 1:7–8; emphasis added).

To those who love God, Nahum said, He is good. Gracious. Patient. Forgiving. Those who trust in Him can run to Him and find refuge.

But to those who spurn His love, flaunt their sin, and ignore His calls for repentance, He is fearsome and terrifying. Although Nineveh had repented during Jonah's time, their repentance didn't last. Nahum prophesied the city's destruction because they had again turned their backs on God.

"The LORD is a jealous and avenging God;" Nahum warned the wicked Assyrians, "the LORD takes vengeance and is filled with wrath. The LORD takes vengeance on his foes and vents his wrath against his enemies.

"The LORD is slow to anger but great in power; the LORD will not leave the guilty unpunished. His way is in the whirlwind and the storm, and clouds are the dust of his feet" (vv. 2–3).

But for Judah, His chosen people, Nahum painted a very different face of God:

"Look, there on the mountains, the feet of one who brings good news, who proclaims peace!" (v. 15).

So it is for us today. God is patient, not willing that any should perish, but that all should come to repentance (2 Peter 3:9). But one day His patience will come to an end. He will be forced to judge those who have spurned His love and rejected the salvation His Son, Jesus, purchased on the cross.

Judge Gardner wouldn't have been a righteous judge if he'd let me trample the integrity of the court by treating it carelessly. It was in my best interest to respond to his gracious invitation with humility and respect.

God wouldn't be a righteous judge if He allowed mankind to trample the sacrificial love He demonstrated on the cross by treating it carelessly. It's always in our best interests to respond to God's gracious invitation with humility and respect.

God wants to save all who will come to Him, but not all will. On judgment day, which face of God will you see?

"The LORD is good, a refuge in times of trouble. He cares for those who trust in him, **but** . . ." (Nahum 1:7–8).

wait

For the revelation awaits an appointed time;
it speaks of the end and will not prove false. Though it linger,
wait for it; it will certainly come and will not delay.

Habakkuk 2:3

Winter lasts forever in New England. We used to say my home state of Rhode Island has three seasons, not four—June, July, and winter. From the first frost of October to the last frost of May, the landscape shivers under grey skies, damp air, and icy blankets of snow. The growing season is short. Farmers and amateur gardeners often wait until after Memorial Day to sow their seeds and plant their tender plants.

Every year at Easter my mother would gather my sisters and me, dressed in our holiday finery, for a picture. One snapshot stands out in my memory. Taken during the first week of April, the grainy image shows the three of us huddled together in front of our house with purple crocuses poking through the snow at our feet.

I've weathered quite a few long winters. Some I've marked on the calendar, crossing out days with big red *X*s as the months creep by. Others I've marked with tear-filled journal entries and agonizing seasons of prayer.

A prodigal child, a struggling marriage, or a relational conflict can cause even the steadiest hope to wobble. A long season of unemployment or a loved one battling addiction invites Satan's icy fingers to clutch at our hearts and squeeze the breath from our lungs. Years of unanswered prayers for a baby, a spouse, or a dream rattle the leaves of hope, scattering the precious few that cling to the branches.

When you're in the middle of a long winter, spring seems very far away. It's easy to imagine, as C. S. Lewis wrote of the fictional world of Narnia, that it will be "always winter and never Christmas."[9]

This is why I take comfort in these verses in the tiny book of Habakkuk. They remind me that though God's answer seems long in coming, it will come.

The prophet Habakkuk groaned under God's seeming disinterest in the chaos that surrounded him. Evil acts, lawlessness, and injustice troubled his world. "How long, LORD, must I call for help, but you do not listen?" he wailed to the sky. "Or cry out to you, 'Violence!' but you do not save? Why do you make me look at injustice? Why do you tolerate wrongdoing?" (Habakkuk 1:2–3).

I've often prayed Habakkuk-type prayers, asking God, "How long?"

How long will it take for a loved one to recognize the self-destructive path they're on and repent? How long will the godly suffer with no one to rescue them? How long will people struggle with cancer, Parkinson's, or depression before they experience a breakthrough?

"Look at the nations and watch," the Lord replies to Habakkuk's question, "and be utterly amazed. For I am going to do something in your days that you would not believe, even if you were told" (v. 5).

God reminded Habakkuk that though answers seem slow in coming, he could trust His timing. And he could trust that the means God used would accomplish His good and perfect will, even when they weren't what he expected.

Long before my sisters and I glimpsed the crocus petals pushing through the snow that Easter day, God was at work.

When last year's blossoms died, He'd already begun the process of rebirth.

All seemed frozen and dead to the watching world. But God was working where we couldn't see. First the roots emerged, drinking in life-giving water, and pushing deep into the icy soil. Then the leaves unfurled. Finally the stalk pushed through the snow. "Though it linger, wait for it," God said to Habakkuk. "It will certainly come and will not delay" (2:3).

Then, one snowy day no different from all the rest, beauty erupted from the ground.

And we marveled.

Crocuses in the snow.

You may have sown the seeds of faith into your children, but the soil of their heart seems frozen solid. Perhaps you've planted snips of kindness into relationships that shiver with cold. Maybe you've watered the ground with your prayer-soaked tears, but the landscape stretches before you like a polar expanse.

Don't give up. Believe that the God who is always at work is working for you. Sight unseen. Accomplishing His purposes, in His way, in His timing.

"The LORD is in his holy temple," Habakkuk declares (v. 20). "The just shall live by his faith" (v. 4 NKJV).

Trust in the Lord. Don't give up hope. **Wait**.

humility

Seek the LORD, all you humble of the land, you who do what
he commands. Seek righteousness, seek humility.

Zephaniah 2:3

I've never considered myself a prideful person. My average intel-
ligence, average appearances, and average list of accomplishments
have seldom inspired delusions of grandeur.

Yet as we learned in the devotion from Obadiah, pride wears
many masks.

I found one of these masks, of all places, in my prayer closet. God
revealed it to me through the prophet Zephaniah.

In the Old Testament book that bears his name, Zephaniah called
to God's people, encouraging them to seek the Lord. He referred to
them as "all you humble of the land" (2:3). They were the remnant,
those who followed the Lord and walked according to His ways.

I identify with the people of Judah, because I, too, seek to obey
God in a culture that seems determined to move further and further
away from God.

"Seek righteousness," Zephaniah exhorted them. "Seek humility" (v. 3).

I held my life up to Zephaniah's standard and gave myself a pass. I try to do what's right. I try to walk humbly.

What about your prayer life? the Spirit of the Lord whispered. *Do you seek humility as you pray?*

Seek humility as I pray?

I thought we were to come boldly to the throne of God. Ask Him to move mountains. Search out His promises and wave them before Him like an IOU until He has to deliver.

Seek humility?

In my prayers?

What does this look like? How do I pray boldly—and in faith (because those verses are in the Bible too)—yet with humility?

Jesus was humble, the Spirit spoke again.

Jesus, who, of anyone who ever lived, had the greatest right to demand His way. Jesus, who had the power of heaven and earth at His disposal and could call ten thousand angels to rescue Him. Jesus, who sweat great drops of blood because, in His humanity, He didn't want to drink the full cup of God's wrath for our sin.

Jesus, who prayed, "My Father, if it is possible, may this cup be taken from me. Yet not as I will, but as you will" (Matthew 26:39).

By surrendering His will to God's, Jesus demonstrated what humility in prayer looks like. He fell on His holy, perfect, sinless face and surrendered His human wishes so God could accomplish eternal glory.

He bowed His humanity before His Father's divinity and declared, "No matter how bad the circumstances are or what I'm feeling, I trust you."

Many others have modeled a similar trust.

Abraham, raising his knife to sacrifice his son, declared, "God himself will provide the lamb" (Genesis 22:8).

Job, suffering the loss of everything he treasured, cried out, "Though he slay me, yet will I hope in him" (Job 13:15).

Martha, bowed by grief over the brother Jesus could've healed but didn't, confessed, "I believe that you are the Messiah, the Son of God, who is to come into the world" (John 11:27).

Paul, shipwrecked, beaten, stoned, and imprisoned, wrote, "I consider that our present sufferings are not worth comparing with the glory that will be revealed in us" (Romans 8:18).

As I answer Zephaniah's call to seek humility in my prayers, I walk in the footsteps of those who have yielded their wills to a will greater than theirs. To a Father who is all-knowing, merciful, full of compassion and love. To a trustworthy God who orders the events of every day for our good and His glory.

Because Scripture does not lie, I can come boldly to the throne of grace and find help in time of need (Hebrews 4:16), but God also calls me to come humbly.

In my family, Lord, may your will be done.

In my health, Lord, may your will be done.

In my finances, Lord, may your will be done.

In my future, Lord, may your will be done.

Tomorrow, when we go into our prayer closets, may we, like Jesus, bow before the Lord Almighty—in righteousness and **humility**.

consider

Now, therefore, thus says the LORD of hosts:
Consider your ways.

Haggai 1:5 ESV

When a friend asked if I'd be willing to dog sit her Boston terrier, Boomer, I jumped at the chance.

"At last," I said. "Someone will finally get to use our doggy door." We'd lost our beloved rescue, Winston, just weeks before moving into our new home. The doggy door that so conveniently led from our back porch into the yard had stood unused for almost four years.

"Boomer will love that," my friend said when she dropped him off. "We have a doggy door at home, and he goes in and out all the time. Ours is on the left side of the door, and yours is on the right, but he'll figure it out."

That night, after Boomer ate his evening meal, I opened the kitchen door leading to the porch.

"Go on out, Boomer," I said. Boomer knew *out*, and he took off running—straight into the wooden panel on the *left* side of the screen door. He shook his head, backed up, and tried it again. *Crash.* Straight into the panel.

"Over here, Boomer," I gestured, tapping the doggy door on the right. "This is the way out." Lifting the flap with one hand and grabbing Boomer by the collar, I shoved him through the opening and into the back yard.

I'd like to say Boomer was a quick learner, but I can't. Four times a day for four days he charged out onto the back porch straight into the wooden panel to the left of the door. There was no convincing him that wasn't the way out. His doggy door at home was on the left, and by golly, the one at my house was too.

Except it wasn't.

I shake my head at Boomer's stubborn refusal to learn, but I see a lot of Boomer in me. How many times have I responded selfishly to my husband and caused a rift in our relationship? Or said yes to something I should have said no to and regretted it later? How many times have I blurted out the first thought that came to mind and suffered the consequences of my tactlessness?

Like Boomer, I could spare myself a lot of headaches and heartaches if I'd consider my ways and change my approach.

The prophet Haggai preached a similar message to the Jews who had returned to Jerusalem after the seventy-year exile in Babylon. Coming to their homeland with clear instructions from God to rebuild the temple, they began well. They built an altar and a foundation, but when pressure from opposing neighbors sidelined the project, construction ceased. Even after the emperor of Persia lifted the restrictions, they chose not to continue.

They resettled the city, planted their fields, and built elaborate homes for themselves, but ignored God's call. Like Boomer stubbornly refusing to follow my instructions, they persisted in doing what they thought was best, with disastrous results.

"Consider your ways," the Lord called through Haggai. "You have sown much, and harvested little. You eat, but you never have enough; you drink, but you never have your fill. You clothe yourselves, but no one is warm. And he who earns wages does so to put them into a bag with holes" (Haggai 1:6–7 ESV).

"Consider your ways," the Lord called a second time. "Go up to the hills and bring wood and build the house, that I may take pleasure in it and that I may be glorified, says the LORD. You looked for much, and behold, it came to little. And when you brought it home, I blew it away. Why? declares the LORD of hosts. Because of my house that lies in ruins, while each of you busies himself with his own house" (vv. 7–9 ESV).

God hasn't called us to grab a saw and a hammer to build His physical temple, but we are called to build His spiritual house by accomplishing His work in the world. To do this, we must consider our ways and put Him first.

Jesus reinforced this truth when He said, "But seek *first* the kingdom of God and his righteousness, and all these things will be added to you" (Matthew 6:33; emphasis added).

Are you experiencing frustration and a lack of success in some area of your life? Perhaps this is because your priorities don't align with God's. Do you honor Him first with your words, actions, and thoughts? Or have you put your agenda and desires ahead of His? Do you put so much time and energy into the temporary things of this world that you've neglected the eternal?

Boomer failed to consider his ways and continued to smash his head against the doggy door that wasn't there. We don't have to continue to smash our heads against the truth that God's priorities, not ours, are best. While Boomer never experienced the joy of a headache-free exit, we can experience the joy of putting God first and watching Him work in our lives. Best of all, as we order our days according to His priorities, He will "take pleasure in it and be honored" (Haggai 1:8).

"Consider from this day onward," God said. "From this day on I will bless you" (2:18–19 ESV).

Whenever we're tempted to put our agenda ahead of God's, may we remember that God blesses those who put Him first. As we live in submission to Him, may we never fail to **consider**.

small

Do not despise these small beginnings,
for the LORD rejoices to see the work begin.
Zechariah 4:10 NLT

As the editor of a regional Christian magazine, I often attended conferences where I met with writers from around the country. Sometimes they'd ask me to critique their work; other times they wanted to pitch an article or an idea.

At one conference, a woman approached me with a shy smile and a hopeful gleam in her eyes. Her words came out in a rush, as if she'd been holding her breath. "I saw on the website that you edit a Christian magazine, so I made it my goal to meet with you here at the conference. I'd like to submit something."

"Good for you," I said. "Tell me what you write about."

"Oh, I'm a baby writer," she said. "I'm just beginning."

"Great!" I said. "I love babies."

We laughed, and the conversation flowed easily from there. It was only after I'd returned to my hotel room and reflected on the day that I realized that of all the words I'd spoken that day, my response to that writer was probably the most Godlike.

Why? Because God loves babies too. He loves small things. He loves beginnings.

He revealed this in the small Old Testament book of Zechariah. The Israelites had just returned from exile in Babylon, and God had given them an assignment—rebuild His temple. The First Temple, Solomon's temple, had been an architectural, cultural, and historical marvel. The finest cedar comprised its walls, shining gold covered the floor, and elaborate tapestries hung from its ceilings. The plunder from King David's conquests and the wealth from Solomon's treasury had funded its construction. It was glorious.

But that temple was gone—destroyed by the Babylonians seventy years earlier. All that remained was a heap of rubble, piles of charred stone, and a motley group of exiles who had straggled back to their homeland to pick up the pieces.

In Haggai 2:3, the Lord acknowledges the people's discouragement and asks through Haggai, "Who of you is left who saw this house in its former glory? How does it look to you now? Does it not seem to you like nothing?"

Even though God knew the Second Temple would be but a shadow of the former, He didn't disparage it. And He didn't allow the people to either.

"Do not despise these small beginnings," God encouraged, "for the LORD rejoices to see the work begin" (Zechariah 4:10 NLT). In other words, I love babies. Baby steps. Baby talk. And baby beginnings.

Scripture proves this. World-altering events sprang from small beginnings.

God began the human race with one man made out of dust. A very small beginning.

He began the nation of Israel with a one-hundred-year-old man and a postmenopausal woman.

He began the ministry of the long-awaited Messiah in a tiny village called Bethlehem.

He began the incarnation of the Godhead in a tiny baby boy.

He began the task of evangelizing the world with a dozen ragtag disciples.

And He began the indwelling of the Holy Spirit in a small number of disciples who committed themselves to pray and fast.

The young writer who sat across from me at the conference disparaged her small beginning, but God didn't. He celebrated it.

What small beginning has God planted in your heart? Set in motion in your life? Do you, like my writer friend, want to write a book? Lead a Bible study? Share your faith? Start a business? Prioritize your physical health? Get out of debt? Learn to play an instrument? Travel? Kick a bad habit? Read your Bible more?

Begin today. Start where you are, and don't disparage it. Like God, recognize that some of the greatest endeavors begin with something **small**.

remembrance

Then those who feared the LORD talked with each other,
and the LORD listened and heard. A scroll of remembrance
was written in his presence concerning those
who feared the LORD and honored his name.

Malachi 3:16

Heartbreak has the power to steal the color from our world. Days that sparkled with sunshine grieve under funeral drapes. Months that flowed with seasonal color now swirl in inky black.

When grief, trials, or loss paint our world with the broad brush of sorrow, we wonder if it pays to follow God. Have we served Him in vain? Does He care that we suffer? Do our virtuous acts matter?

The people of Malachi's day asked these questions. They lamented over the hardships and struggles that plagued their lives and declared, "It is futile to serve God. What do we gain by carrying out his requirements and going about like mourners before the LORD Almighty?" (Malachi 3:14).

When our children choose a different path than the one we set them on, we wonder if it mattered that we took them to church, taught them Bible verses, and folded their little hands to pray. When our marriage sputters and grows cold, we question whether Christian unions have any greater chance of success than secular ones. When we groan under the same cancers, addictions, betrayals, and death as those who spurn God or proclaim He doesn't exist, we question whether faith matters. Does it profit us to keep His commands?

Sometimes our discouragement overwhelms us, and our love for God grows cold. We become cynical and wounded by the trials in our lives. As the Israelites did for centuries, we turn away from God. Whether we do so with fanfare and boldly walk away or leave so quietly that no one notices, God knows. "Ever since the time of your ancestors you have turned away from my decrees and have not kept them," God declared to the people of Malachi's day (v. 7).

Yet God didn't give up on them. And He doesn't give up on us. His love isn't dependent on our faithfulness, but on His. We don't deserve His mercy, yet He freely lavishes it on us. We can never earn His love, yet He extends it to us every day.

My friend Katrina's son Woods went through a challenging period of childish independence. He declared his autonomy from her often—and loudly. Sometimes he refused to submit to her rules and threw tantrums in the most public of places.

One day, while visiting my home, he flung himself to the floor.

"No!" he wailed. "I don't want to go." He flailed. He kicked. He sobbed. When Katrina stooped to gather him in her arms, he pushed her away.

"I don't like you," he declared with tears streaming from his eyes. "I don't like you. I don't like you. I don't like you."

Katrina wrapped her arms around him and held him close. She tucked his head under her chin and began to rock. "You may not like me right now," she said, "but I love you."

In the days of Malachi, the Lord gathered disobedient Israel into His mighty arms and whispered a similar declaration of love into their ears. "I the LORD do not change. So you, the descendants of Jacob, are not destroyed" (v. 6). His covenant love for Jacob (and for us) didn't depend on their hearts, but on His.

Long before He called His people to himself, He set His love on them. He knew they would shine in courageous faith and flounder in sin and unbelief. They'd love Him and doubt Him, sometimes simultaneously. Their failures didn't catch Him by surprise, nor did their faithless moments retract His promises. The same is true for us today.

"Then those who feared the LORD talked with each other," Malachi wrote, "and the LORD listened and heard. A scroll of remembrance was written in his presence concerning those who feared the LORD and honored his name" (v. 16).

A scroll of remembrance. A record of every act of kindness we do and every fledgling faith step we take. A list of the times we've honored Him and loved others. A note of every prayer we've prayed and every time we've made Him smile.

God doesn't keep this scroll of remembrance to tally the good and bad for judgment day or to decide who merits His favor. He writes the scroll because He delights in us. We are His "treasured possession" (v. 17).

As Katrina did to her son, God declared His love to the faltering children of Israel. His words trickle down through the ages and soothe our trembling hearts.

The Day of the Lord will bring judgment to those who have spurned God's love, but it will bring great reward to those who have loved and served Him—even those who have served Him imperfectly (and that's all of us).

"'On the day when I act,' says the LORD Almighty, 'they will be my treasured possession'" (v. 17).

Today, if you're struggling with heartache and wondering if it's useless to serve God, turn your heart toward Him in faith. Rest in His unmerited favor. Trust in His steadfast love. And be encouraged that our gracious God sees your faithfulness and records all the ways you honor Him in His scroll of **remembrance**.

rest

Come to me, all you who are weary and burdened, and I will give you rest. Take my yoke upon you and learn from me, for I am gentle and humble in heart, and you will find rest for your souls.

Matthew 11:28–29

When our kids were young, we couldn't afford many vacations, so we went camping instead. It didn't cost much to rent a spot in a state park, and South Carolina was full of them.

I soon discovered that while camping didn't cost much, a successful trip required lots of time and effort. We researched locations and made reservations. I planned a menu and shopped for food and supplies for the weekend. I packed every cooking implement I needed to make three meals a day.

Then we researched fun side trips and activities we could do near the campground. We mapped out the route and filled the car with gas. By the time we drove to the park, set up camp, and prepared our first meal, I was exhausted. Camping was fun, but it wasn't restful.

The year after our youngest daughter graduated from homeschool high school, David announced, "I want to take you somewhere to celebrate all the hard work you've done educating the girls. Where would you like to go?"

"I've always wanted to go on a cruise."

The day before we set sail, I packed my suitcase. The day of, we showed up, presented our ticket, and boarded the ship. "If you're hungry," a steward said, "they're serving lunch at Guy's Burger Bar."

For five days, someone other than myself fed me, transported me, and planned my activities. They washed my dishes, cooked my meals, and entertained me. Each night, I'd return to our room to discover a new towel animal on my bed. The only decision I had to make was whether to choose chocolate lava cake or Baked Alaska.

For many years, my Christian life was more like camping than cruising. I knew from the start I couldn't earn God's favor, nor could I deserve it. I embraced Ephesians 2:8–9, "For it is by grace you have been saved, through faith—and this is not from yourselves, it is the gift of God—not by works, so that no one can boast."

I knew salvation was a gift, but for many years I failed to realize that my ability to live the Christian life is also a gift—by faith, apart from works.

The church I attended added to my confusion. "If you don't do more, give more, and serve more every year," I heard from the pulpit, "then you're not a good Christian."

So I did more. I gave more. I served more. Like a teacher filling out a school progress report, I'd evaluate the previous year and compare how I'd done. Volunteered for vacation Bible school *and* the bus ministry. Check. Increased our giving to missions. Check. Hosted a visiting pastor and his wife. Check.

Then our daughter was born. Our precious, exhausting, expensive daughter. Her crib replaced the guest bed. Her hospital bills ate into our missions giving. Her colic and separation anxiety kept me from serving in the bus ministry. Some nights I'd fall into bed too exhausted to spend time in my Bible or pray.

I was failing at the Christian life. God had to be disappointed with me. I wasn't checking off the list.

Then I read Matthew 11:28–29, "Come to me, all you who are weary and burdened, and I will give you rest. Take my yoke upon you and learn from me, for I am gentle and humble in heart, and you will find rest for your souls."

In a moment of spiritual clarity, I realized that somewhere between "I surrender all," and "I want to live for you," I'd missed something important: The same effortless grace that saved me would also make it possible for me to live the Christian life.

Instead of striving, I thanked God that He promised to empower me through the Holy Spirit to do His will.

I no longer checked off boxes on an imaginary twenty-point list of how to live for God. Instead, I learned to trust God to lead me, each day, to do what pleased Him, which included faithfully studying the Bible, praying, and serving. But even in this I could rest in His power to be faithful. I was free to trust Him for the details of how and where He wanted me to live out my faith each day.

After almost a decade of striving to please God, I rested in the good work He had begun in me and would continue to do (Philippians 1:6). I cast off the yoke of performance and accepted the yoke of grace. "Teach me to do your will," I prayed. "Empower me to do the good work you've planned for me. Lead me into the life-giving rest you promise."

If you're exhausted from trying to be everything you wish you could be for God, lay down the yoke of performance. Take up the yoke of grace. As it settles softly on your shoulders, breathe in God's favor and breathe out His peace. Accept what Christ has done for you. Trust what He will continue to do. Embrace God's gift of spiritual **rest**.

alone

When he was alone with his own disciples,
he explained everything.

Mark 4:34

In a world of a thousand devices, are we ever truly alone?

Technology invites people into our living rooms from half a world away. A dozen apps bring podcasters, broadcasters, strangers, and friends as close as the phones that live in our pockets. We have unrestricted access to the world and spend our days at the mercy of a thousand dings. Even the Do Not Disturb setting on our phone permits a chosen few to awaken us from sleep or interrupt our quiet moments.

Alone time, even if no one is physically near, is rare.

Jesus and his disciples didn't carry cell phones, but they, too, struggled to be alone. Crowds pressed in on them. The sick, lame, and demon possessed filled the homes and streets and desert places where they served. Ministry demands interrupted their sleep and disturbed their prayer times.

Mark 4 describes one of those days. As they walked, people pressed in, made requests, and demanded attention. The crush of the crowd pinned Jesus between the sand and the sea, so he climbed into a boat and pushed off from shore. There He found breathing room. The expanse of water between Him and the people created a natural megaphone to project His voice, and He began to teach.

"Listen! A farmer went out to sow his seed" (v. 3).

His disciples, like the listening audience, heard Jesus's words, but a thousand distractions outshouted them. Their brains were engaged, but their understanding was darkened. Like glimpsing a present between wrapping paper edges that don't quite meet, they saw a hint of the treasure He had for them but had no clue what it was. Only later, when they had sent the crowds away and gathered at His feet, did true enlightenment come.

"When he was alone with his own disciples, he explained everything" (v. 34).

Jesus needed to spend time alone with His disciples. He also needed to spend time with His Father. Although He was fully God, He was also fully man. For a time, He had temporarily set aside the voluntary use of His deity. He sought God's wisdom, direction, and understanding as we do. Luke 5:16 tells us He "often withdrew to lonely places and prayed." Other times, "very early in the morning, while it was still dark, Jesus got up, left the house and went off to a solitary place, where he prayed" (Mark 1:35).

Two thousand years have passed, but the truth remains—we can catch a glimmer of the gift under the wrapping paper as we whoosh by, but until we sit at Jesus's feet and allow Him to unwrap it for us, it will remain a mystery.

I confess that I often survive on between-the-paper glimpses. Long to-do lists woo me away from my spot at Jesus's feet. The siren call to get moving, do more, and don't stop pulls me from the depths of biblical insight to the shallow waters of surface knowledge.

Yet when I linger with Him alone, He spreads a table before me.

If you're done with gazing at the wrapping paper and are ready to open the gift, why not sneak away with Jesus? Sit at His feet. Read His Word. Listen to His voice.

Make time to be **alone**.

blessed

Looking at his disciples, he said: "Blessed are you who are poor, for yours is the kingdom of God. Blessed are you who hunger now, for you will be satisfied. Blessed are you who weep now, for you will laugh. Blessed are you when people hate you, when they exclude you and insult you and reject your name as evil, because of the Son of Man. Rejoice in that day and leap for joy, because great is your reward in heaven. For that is how their ancestors treated the prophets."

Luke 6:20–23

As a writer, I take words seriously. I spend hours choosing just the right ones and arranging them in a particular order. I take into account nuances in meaning, connotation, and usage. Sometimes I pore over a thesaurus seeking a single word that captures a thousand shades of meaning and perfectly expresses what I want to say with no room for misunderstanding.

If a character in one of my stories is laid out in bed sick with a raging headache, excruciating body aches, and a fever higher than a hot-air balloon at an air show, I'm not going to describe him as *under the weather.* More like *nearly under the ground,* as in *six feet under.*

My love for just the right words is why I stumbled over Jesus's list of those who are blessed in His Sermon on the Mount. If I were editing the list of adjectives Jesus used, the first six He chose would have sent me to a dictionary for replacements: Poor? Hungry? Weeping? Hated? Excluded? Insulted? Really, Jesus? They don't sound blessed to me. They sound miserable.

And yet He chose these words:

Poor—spiritually destitute. No hope. No spiritual currency to barter with. No means to cancel the sin debt levied against us.

Hungry—craving but never full. Always yearning, longing, and desiring.

Weeping—emotionally destitute. Mourning the loss of a loved one, a marriage, health, wealth, or a relationship.

Hated—excluded, insulted.

If I'd written Jesus's sermon, my adjective choices to describe the blessed might have sounded more like: Rich. Satisfied. Happy. Loved. Accepted. Affirmed.

And herein lies the struggle between our ways and God's ways.

We want to take the short cuts, the easy roads, the autobahn of life. We want no pain and no struggle. We'd like God to open our souls and pour in spiritual muscle instead of having to pump iron in the gym called life.

But this isn't the way God works. Christ says to be spiritually rich we must recognize our spiritual poverty. Before we can be satisfied, we must ache with hunger for God. To laugh—a great, big belly laugh of the redeemed—we must first weep in repentance over our sin. To be included in God's family, we must risk being ostracized. To be exalted, we must be abased.

So many of Jesus's teachings are oxymoronic. They fling the logic of this world to the wind and call us to a higher way. "You want to be first?" He said to His disciples, "then be last." "You want the seat of honor? Take the chair in the corner. You want to live abundantly? Then prepare to die."

Jesus knew that for everything we surrender in His name, we'll receive from Him so much more. In this life, and in the life to come (Luke 18:29–30).

Spiritual beggars become children of the king. Grieving souls laugh and dance. Hungry disciples slide up to the heavenly banquet table and feast to their hearts' content.

Instead of gorging on the fleeting riches of this world and choking on pseudo abundance, we can confidently rest in the poverty of spirit. We can stretch out needy hands to the Father and watch Him fill them to overflowing—with himself.

It is the narrow way. The lonely way. The Jesus way that leads to the cross and ends in a resurrection.

Few find it. Yet when they do, they are truly **blessed**.

grace

For from his fullness we have all received, grace upon grace.

John 1:16 ESV

One of the greatest heartbreaks of my six-year-old life happened half a block from our apartment in North Providence, Rhode Island.

Every summer afternoon around three o'clock, my friends and I listened for the jingle of Jimmy the ice cream man's bell. We'd hear the first note as his truck rounded the corner to climb the long hill to our neighborhood. We'd run home, beg our moms for money, and gather on the sidewalk. Ten cents bought a popsicle, fifteen was enough for a one-scoop cone, and a quarter would buy a double scoop of sweet deliciousness. Glory hallelujah.

That fateful day in August began like all the others. Hear the bell. Dash home. Beg for money. Gather on the sidewalk.

"What may I get for you, young lady?" Jimmy asked, white hair poking out from under his hat, ice cream scoop at the ready.

I'm sure my face reflected the struggle within me. Raspberry sherbet or maple walnut? Maple walnut or raspberry sherbet?

"One scoop of raspberry sherbet in a sugar cone, please."

He opened the case, dug deeply into the tub of ice cream, and handed over my treat.

"Here you go, little lady. Enjoy."

I clutched the top-heavy cone, took one luxurious lick, and stepped back to make room for the next eager customer. One foot, then the other hit the tire of my bicycle. In a rush to beat everyone to the front of the line, I'd flung it on the ground near the truck. Slow-motion momentum carried me backward until I landed on the bike with a crash.

My ice cream cone flew into the air and landed, upended and covered with dirt, beside me.

Neighbors two blocks away heard the wail that erupted from the deepest part of my ice-cream-loving soul. My mother heard it, too, and met me at the door of our apartment. She gathered me in her arms, checked for broken bones, and tried to decipher my hiccupy sobs.

Before she could console me, we heard a knock at the door. My friend Freddy, forehead wrinkled in concern, stood on the stoop. In his hand was a double scoop, not a single, of raspberry sherbet—in a sugar cone.

"Jimmy said to give this to you. He hopes you're okay."

I remember Jimmy the ice cream man every time I read John 1:16 (ESV): "For from his fullness we have all received, grace upon grace."

For many years, my understanding of the term *grace* was slippery. One of the first verses I memorized as a new believer contained the word. "For by *grace* you have been saved through faith. And this is not your own doing; it is the gift of God, not a result of works, so that no one may boast" (Ephesians 2:8–9 ESV). My pastor called this type of grace "undeserved favor." We can do nothing to earn or deserve salvation. God bestows it on sinful people because He loves us.

As time went on, I heard *grace* used in other contexts:

"God will give you the grace to get through this."

"God's grace enabled me to do what was right."

"When I thought I couldn't do what God had called me to do, His grace empowered me."

I'd eagerly embraced grace for salvation, but I didn't understand grace for living. Once God saved me, I assumed it was up to me to muddle through the rest of my Christian life. My willpower would have to enable me to say no to sin. My determination must help me grow as a believer. My strength had to empower me to do the hard things life demanded.

You can imagine how well that turned out.

Then, glory hallelujah, I learned about another type of grace—sanctifying grace.

Sanctifying grace, the power that enables us to become more like Jesus, works in us in four ways:

Sanctifying grace enables us to say no to sin.

"For we do not have a high priest who is unable to empathize with our weaknesses, but we have one who has been tempted in every way, just as we are—yet he did not sin. Let us then approach God's throne of grace with confidence, so that we may receive mercy and find grace to help us in our time of need" (Hebrews 4:15–16).

Sanctifying grace empowers us to confess and forsake sin and receive His forgiveness when we fail.

"If we confess our sins, he is faithful and just and will forgive us our sin and purify us from all unrighteousness" (1 John 1:9).

Sanctifying grace helps us do the good works God has planned for us.

"And God is able to make all grace abound to you, so that having all sufficiency in all things at all times, you may abound in every good work" (2 Corinthians 9:8 ESV).

Sanctifying grace helps us endure emotional, spiritual, and physical pain.

The apostle Paul, plagued by some type of physical or spiritual weakness, testified, "Three times I pleaded with the Lord about this, that it should leave me. But he said to me, 'My grace is sufficient for you, for my power is made perfect in weakness.' Therefore I will boast all the more gladly of my weaknesses, so that the power of Christ may rest upon me" (2 Corinthians 12:8–9 ESV).

The day I tumbled over my bike and dumped my scoop of ice cream in the dirt was a sad day. I didn't deserve the second cone Jimmy the ice cream man sent through my friend Freddy. And I certainly didn't deserve a double scoop of the raspberry sherbet—in a sugar cone.

Years later, the day I understood the wretched condition of my sin-filled soul was a pivotal day. I didn't deserve the scoop of saving grace God sent through His Son, Jesus. And I certainly didn't deserve the sanctifying second scoop, "grace upon grace," God lavished on me.

Jimmy the ice cream man's grace made my day better. God's grace transformed my life. By the twin gifts of saving and sanctifying grace, God gave me life and life more abundant (John 10:10). Because of this double portion, I can sing with John Newton, the converted former slave trader turned preacher, "'Tis grace hath brought me safe thus far, and grace will lead me home."

Amazing **grace**.

witnesses

For many days he was seen by those who had
traveled with him from Galilee to Jerusalem.
They are now his witnesses to our people.

Acts 13:31

When the terrifying events of 9/11 occurred, Katie was twelve years old. Her family watched as President George W. Bush stood upon the ashes of the World Trade Center with a bullhorn in his hand and addressed New York City's first responders. "I can hear you. I can hear you. The rest of the world hears you. And the people who knocked these buildings down will hear all of us soon."

When President Bush was reelected, Katie's friend Hannah and her family invited her to attend his second inauguration with them. On a snowy day in Washington, along with one hundred thousand others, they watched him take the presidential oath of office.

On December 20, 2010, Katie finally had the opportunity to meet President Bush and his wife, Laura. Evangelist Billy Graham had invited the former president and first lady to tour the newly opened Billy Graham Library and sign copies of their memoirs.

Katie stood in line for hours outside the library on a cold Friday in December to obtain one of the coveted wristbands required for admission. The next day she waited with more than a thousand admirers to meet him and ask him to sign her copy of their book.

When her turn came, she shook his hand, gave him her book to sign, and stepped aside to make room for the next person.

But the former president was kind. And patient. "Now hold on there, little lady," he said. "What's your name?" They talked for a moment before he thanked her for coming and turned to the next person in line.

When she returned home that day, Katie's eyes sparkled, and her words tumbled out. She had seen George W. Bush, shaken his hand, and talked with him. She couldn't wait to tell her friends she'd met the former president of the United States.

She never dreamed they wouldn't believe her.

"George W. Bush did not come to Charlotte," Alana said with a snort, "and you did not meet him."

"Nice try, Katie," her friend Mark said, "but I'm not buying it. Even if he did come to Charlotte—and why would he want to?— there's no way Secret Service would let you get within a mile of him."

Even her beloved Uncle Pete was skeptical—until she shared the Fox News article describing the gathering.[10] "The book signing event sold out in a matter of hours Saturday. Library officials would not say how many people obtained the wristbands necessary for admission. But they began lining up outside the library at dawn." The story confirmed the details of Katie's account—details she couldn't have known if she hadn't been an eyewitness.

Seven times in the book of Acts, the word *witnesses* is used to describe the men and women who testified to others about Jesus.

"God has raised this Jesus to life, and we are all *witnesses* of it," Peter said as he addressed the crowd (Acts 2:32).

"We are witnesses of these things, and so is the Holy Spirit, whom God has given to those who obey him," he said as he stood outside the temple and taught (5:32).

"But God raised him from the dead on the third day and caused him to be seen. He was not seen by all the people, but by *witnesses* whom God had already chosen—by us who ate and drank with him after he rose from the dead" (10:40–41).

Scripture (and extrabiblical sources) record how Jesus appeared to the women at the tomb, to his twelve disciples, to five hundred men at one time, and to the apostles James and Paul. These early disciples weren't passing along "cleverly devised fables," as some suspected. They were testifying to what they had seen with their eyes, heard with their ears, and touched with their fingers. They had walked and talked with the resurrected Christ. They witnessed His appearances. Many were martyred because of their testimonies.

As Katie's friends (and Uncle Pete) could trust her account of the events that happened at the Billy Graham Library on December 20, 2010, because she was an eyewitness among a thousand other eyewitnesses, so we can trust the testimony of the apostles, disciples, and other eyewitnesses as recorded in Scripture. Jewish law stated that a matter could be decided based on the testimony of two witnesses. God provided more than five hundred to testify of the truth of the resurrection.

Salvation, Scripture tells us, comes by faith, and faith comes by the Word of God, but the faith God calls us to isn't a blind leap in the dark. It's a faith based on fact and the indisputable testimony of hundreds of **witnesses.**

all

Consequently, just as one trespass resulted in condemnation
for all people, so also one righteous act resulted
in justification and life for all people.

Romans 5:18

Ryan called it a simple prank, but his fraternity brothers knew otherwise. His plan to paint graffiti on the rival frat house started out as big talk with no action, but that soon changed. The more he boasted about how he was "going to show them," the more determined he became to actually do it. "They've disrespected us one too many times," he said. "It's time to take action."

Joshua, one of the more serious members of the fraternity, tried to reason with him. "All that's going to do is make them more obnoxious," he said. "And get you in trouble. Don't be stupid."

But there was no convincing him. Off he went one night with a backpack full of spray paint.

The next morning, Gus, the frat house manager, called a meeting. Ryan was one of the last to drag himself into the common room, hair disheveled and rubbing sleep from his eyes.

"There's been a report from one of the other houses that members of our fraternity spray-painted their house last night."

Silence.

"Do any of you know anything about this?"

More silence.

Ryan stretched, yawned, and shrugged "What makes 'em think we did it? Coulda been any one of the fraternities."

"Coulda been," he said, "but I doubt someone from another house would've painted Sigma Nu all over it."

"Maybe we were framed," Ryan mumbled.

"Or maybe not," Gus said. "If someone doesn't come forward and accept responsibility, I'm going to hold the whole house responsible. I'll give you three hours to come clean." He stalked from the room and slammed the door behind him.

The guys waited for the sound of his footsteps to recede before they started shouting.

"Ryan, we told you that was a stupid thing to do."

"You graffitied the house with our symbols?" another said. "How dumb is that?"

"Now we're all in trouble," a freckle-faced guy in jogging shorts said. "You'd better turn yourself in. We're not getting punished for your stupid prank."

"I can't turn myself in," Ryan said. "I'm already on probation. One more strike, and I'm out. My dad would kill me, and my mom would cry for a month."

Finally Joshua spoke up. "Let me talk to Gus. Maybe we can work something out." Half an hour later he returned. "Nobody's going to be put on probation."

He turned to Ryan. "The other house agreed to drop the complaint if someone would repaint the house."

Ryan opened his mouth to speak, then closed it again.

"I told them I'd do it," Joshua said. "Gus knows I didn't spray-paint the house, but he doesn't know who did. If you volunteer to paint it, he'll know. He'll kick you out and punish all of us for not ratting on you. I'd rather take the punishment for everyone."

Ryan and Joshua's story, in a small and imperfect way, parallels the scenario that continues to play itself out since Adam and Eve's first days in the garden.

With their resolve weakened by pride and fueled by Satan's lies, the couple chose to disobey God's instructions. Instead of trusting that their heavenly Father had provided everything they needed, they chose to believe Satan's lie—that God was keeping something wonderful from them.

They chose to eat from the one tree in the garden God had declared off-limits—with cataclysmic results. The first half of Romans 5:18 describes it this way: "One trespass resulted in condemnation for all people."

"For all have sinned and fall short of the glory of God," Romans 3:23 agrees with a gavel clap that echoes into eternity. Along with Adam and Eve, we all stand guilty before God. Condemned. Without hope.

When Adam and Eve ate the forbidden fruit, they set in motion a sin cycle that continues to this day. Reproducing like spiritual cancer, their single act has infected a thousand generations. Even today, we eat from Adam and Eve's destructive menu and insist on going our own way.

We doubt God's love. We question His motives. We chafe at His sovereign rule in our lives. Like a toddler challenging his loving father, we mutter under our rebellious breath, "You can't make me."

But God *can* make us—only He chooses not to.

Instead of forcing us to obey Him, He made a way. The glad half of Romans 5:18 follows the sad half: "Consequently, just as one trespass resulted in condemnation for all people, so also one righteous act resulted in justification and life for all people."

Although we don't deserve it—and cannot earn it—Jesus secured for those who will believe in Him the gift of eternal life. His sacrificial death on the cross makes it possible for us to experience freedom from the punishment our sins deserve and enjoy a guilt-free relationship with our heavenly Father.

Ryan's willful act sentenced all his fraternity brothers to guilt and penalty. Joshua's substitutionary punishment secured their pardon. Adam and Eve's rebellious act sentenced all mankind to eternal punishment. Jesus's sacrificial death on the cross secured our justification. If we receive what He did on our behalf by turning from our unbelief and sin and surrendering to Christ, we can stand before God guilt-free.

Are you still living under condemnation for your sin? If you've never asked God to forgive you and surrendered your life to Him, you can do this today. As the multitudes who have come before you, you can approach God with confidence and faith. Christ's righteous act made the gift of eternal life available to all who will believe.

We all stand condemned.

Yet Christ's death was sufficient for **all**.

faithful

Now it is required that those who have been
given a trust must prove faithful.

1 Corinthians 4:2

Pedro's chest puffed with pride, and his smile stretched across his face as he led our family through the hacienda where he worked in Cabo San Lucas, Mexico. He showed us the well-appointed dining room where twenty-one world leaders had met to discuss global economics. He directed us through the luxurious living area where the men had lingered after dinner. Swinging a door open wide, he revealed the master bedroom suite that boasted more square footage than my home.

"This is where the president slept."

He opened the sliding glass doors to reveal a secluded courtyard overlooking the blue-green waters of the Sea of Cortez. He breathed deeply of the salty air and smiled again. "My boss, the owner, visits once or twice a year, but I live here year round. I maintain the property, see to the needs of the household, and make sure the home is ready for guests. It is an honor and a privilege to take care of his beautiful home."

Pedro had been given the responsibility of stewarding the wealth of another. He enjoyed the benefits of the property, but he didn't own it. It had been entrusted into his care.

In a spiritual way, we, like Pedro, are stewards. Instead of physical property, we have been entrusted with a heavenly treasure. Paul says we are "servants of Christ . . . those entrusted with the mysteries God has revealed" (1 Corinthians 4:1).

Entrusted with the mysteries God has revealed.

The word *mystery* appears often in Paul's writings, but Ephesians 5:32 summarizes what this mystery is: "This is a profound mystery—but I am talking about Christ and the church." For millennia, God's people saw hints of His plan to save mankind from our sin and unite Jews and Gentiles into one spiritual body. But they were glimpses only.

Then, in the fullness of time, Christ came. Fully God and fully man, he fulfilled every prophecy that pointed to God's plan of redemption. He knotted every dangling thread on the tapestry of salvation. Then He flipped the masterpiece over for all who had eyes to see. The details of the gospel were hidden no longer.

"He appeared in the flesh, was vindicated by the Spirit, was seen by angels, was preached among the nations, was believed on in the world, was taken up in glory" (1 Timothy 3:16).

Believers are called to be stewards of this mystery. *Faithful* stewards. Caretakers of the trust.

What characteristics do faithful stewards demonstrate? The book of 1 Corinthians spotlights three.

Faithful stewards are focused.

"For I resolved to know nothing while I was with you except Jesus Christ and him crucified" (1 Corinthians 2:2). The overriding message of Paul's day and ours is singularly focused: only Jesus is the way, the truth, and the life. No one comes to God except through Christ (John 14:6). Paul didn't allow the culture of the day or political correctness to water down the essence of the gospel.

Faithful stewards are humble.

"I came to you in weakness with great fear and trembling" (1 Corinthians 2:3). Instead of using the good news of the gospel like a machine gun to blow holes in sin-sick souls, Paul used the message of Christ as a healing balm. He approached needy people as a fellow patient who knew where to go for the cure.

Faithful stewards are Spirit led.

"My message and my preaching were not with wise and persuasive words, but with a demonstration of the Spirit's power, so that your faith might not rest on human wisdom, but on God's power" (vv. 4–5). Paul knew he couldn't rely on his eloquence to bring people to Christ. The Holy Spirit had to do it. He wasn't trying to gather a following for himself, but to encourage others to follow Jesus.

He knew he couldn't argue, bully, or threaten someone into placing their faith in Christ. The Father had to draw them (John 6:44). Only a divine manifestation of God's power could open spiritually blind people's eyes and help them see their need for a Savior.

I marvel that God saves any of us. We can't earn His favor. We don't deserve His grace. But we can express our humble gratitude for the gift of salvation and the life transformation that comes with it.

Pedro worked as a faithful steward for a paycheck. Paul lived a life of focused, humble, Spirit-led devotion to express his love and loyalty to the One who lavished on him the goodness of His grace.

If you know Jesus Christ as Savior and understand the mysteries of God, I pray you'll embrace the honor of stewardship. May God find us **faithful**.

momentary

For our light and momentary troubles are achieving
for us an eternal glory that far outweighs them all.

2 Corinthians 4:17

I suppressed a chuckle when my husband described the panic he felt during an MRI. *That's silly*, I thought. *What's to be anxious about? You just lie there until the test is over.*

I maintained this superior mentality until it was my turn.

As a health care professional, I've watched surgeries that made other people faint and cared for patients with serious health conditions. I've been hospitalized four times. I don't panic in times of crisis and am usually the one calming other people down. But that day at the MRI center, I almost lost it.

The appointment began well. I listened to the instructions the technician gave me about lying still and minimizing movement. "Three scans of ten minutes each," she said. "It'll be over before you know it."

I waved off the washcloth she offered to cover my eyes and hopped up onto the machine. Positioning myself as comfortably as I could, I breathed deeply while she slid me into the long metal cocoon.

That's when my overconfidence undid me. Against the advice of my husband and other friends, I opened my eyes. Two inches above me, suffocatingly close to my face, was the ceiling of the tube. Feeling like a character in a horror movie who'd been buried alive, I squeezed my eyes shut in fright.

A wave of panic like I've never experienced washed over me. My heart raced. My chest rose and fell as I struggled to breathe. Beads of sweat collected on my forehead. My heartbeat swooshed in my ears.

"Lie still, Mrs. Hatcher," the technician's voice encouraged through the speaker beside my ear. "Only five more minutes on the first scan."

If you ask anyone who knows me, they'd say Lori Hatcher is a praying woman. But in that moment, I couldn't pray. Panic banished every coherent thought, leaving me gasping and helpless.

When I was seconds from wriggling myself out of the tube, my spiritual muscle memory kicked in. It reached back forty years to a passage of Scripture I'd memorized as a child with my grandmother. I pictured myself lying beside her on her bed while the words of the Twenty-Third Psalm (NKJV) whispered truth to my frightened heart.

The LORD is my shepherd, I shall not want.

"Only three more minutes on this scan, Mrs. Hatcher," the technician's tinny voice announced.

He makes me to lie down in green pastures.

"We're done with the first scan," the voice said. "Only ten minutes on the next one."

He leads me beside the still waters.

"Five minutes, and you'll be more than halfway there."

He restores my soul.

"Starting the last scan. Just ten quick minutes."

He leads me in the paths of righteousness for His name's sake.

"You're doing great, Mrs. Hatcher."

Yea, though I walk through the valley of the shadow of death, I will fear no evil; for You are with me.

"Five minutes left."

Your rod and Your staff, they comfort me.

I repeated the words to the beloved psalm over and over until quietness and peace calmed my heart. I was almost asleep when I heard the technician's blessed voice through the speaker.

"Okay, Mrs. Hatcher. I'm pulling you out. You're finished."

Reflecting on the experience later (after humbly asking my husband's forgiveness for my lack of sympathy), I identified what had enabled me to endure the fiery trial I'd just experienced: God's Word and the temporary nature of the trial.

The apostle Paul, in his second letter to the Corinthians, described trials far greater than my half-hour stint in the MRI machine. He used the words *hard pressed, perplexed, persecuted, and struck down* (4:8–9). They were "under great pressure, far beyond our ability to endure," to the point that he and his companions "despaired of life itself" (1:8).

What enabled them to hold on? To persevere despite incomprehensible hardships? Our verse for today reveals the answer: They clung to God's Word and the knowledge that everything they endured in light of eternity was "momentary." Compared with the glory that awaits believers, the events of this life are fleeting. A vapor. A trickle in the ocean of forever.

The months of persevering through interpersonal conflict and misunderstanding? A decimal point in the mathematics of heaven.

The years of physical suffering with a chronic disease or condition? A nanosecond in the expanse of eternal life.

The decades of faithful commitment to a challenging marriage? A blip in endless eternity.

The lifelong struggle to serve God, stay pure, and do right in a culture that mocks and disparages believers? A dot on the timeline of forever.

At my friend Ron's funeral, the minister dragged a rope through the front door of the sanctuary and down the center aisle. When he reached the pulpit, it stretched the length of the sanctuary and out the door. He held up one end of the rope so everyone could see the six-inch red tip.

"This tiny red portion of rope is your life on earth. The other part of it—the rope that stretches farther than your eyes can see—is the rest of your life. We have seventy or eighty years on this earth, maybe. We'll spend the rest of our lives in eternity somewhere.

"If we've placed our faith in Jesus Christ, we'll spend eternity with God—in glory that far outweighs anything we have suffered through on this earth. We can take comfort and hope from this."

I remembered his words after my MRI test. By reminding me that my time in the tube was temporary, the technician gave me the perspective I needed to endure. By reminding me of His Word and His promise to care for and sustain me, God gave me the ability to triumph.

My MRI trial didn't achieve for me a weight of eternal glory, but the trials of my life can. If I respond with faith, fix my eyes not "on what is seen, but on what is unseen" (4:18), and press on toward the finish line, the eternal reward I receive in heaven will far outweigh any affliction I endure on earth.

Because God's Word is true, it will be worth it all.

As we cross into the unimaginable perfection of forever and reflect on the hardships of this life, we'll see clearly that our seemingly endless trials, in the grand panorama of God's good plan, were only **momentary**.

infirmity

You know that because of physical infirmity
I preached the gospel to you at the first.

Galatians 4:13 NKJV

My friend Mike began losing his eyesight when he was nine years old. On the day his doctor told him he was going blind, his mother sat him down and said twelve words that charted the course of his life. "There's nothing you can't do if you put your mind to it." He's embraced this philosophy ever since.

Mike shares the teaching responsibilities of our adult Sunday school class with his wife, Jean, who's also blind, and two other (sighted) teachers. As he sips from his extra-large coffee mug and reads from bumpy Brailled pages of notes, he shares deep insights from God's Word.

He doesn't just share his faith within our church, he ministers to the community around him. He's given every Uber driver who's ever transported him a personal invitation to visit our church. He posts

Bible verses and Christian music videos on Facebook and serves as a spiritual mentor to the blind community in our city.

"I don't consider my blindness a curse," Mike said one day at the conclusion of the Sunday school hour. "I consider it a blessing. Everything good in my life has come about because God allowed blindness to enter my life." Instead of chafing at his limitations, Mike embraces the possibilities for ministry they bring.

I thought of Mike when I read the apostle Paul's testimony in Galatians 4:13–14 (NKJV): "You know that because of physical infirmity I preached the gospel to you at the first. And my trial which was in my flesh you did not despise or reject, but you received me as an angel of God, even as Christ Jesus."

Bible scholars have speculated what Paul's infirmity might have been. Some suggest an illness, others suspect he had some type of eye infection or condition that forced him to remain in Galatia. Regardless, Paul didn't view his weakness as a hindrance but as a divinely appointed blessing.

Instead of lamenting that he was stuck in a city he didn't plan to visit battling a physical challenge he'd rather not have, he embraced the opportunity to share the gospel. As a result, many came to faith in Christ. The churches of Antioch, Iconium, Lystra, and Derbe began because of Paul's unexpected time in Galatia.

If you're like me, you prefer to minister from a position of strength. We see physical and emotional challenges as hindrances to successful ministry. But what if we accepted our limitations as custom-designed tools sent from God to enhance, not detract from, our ability to impact those around us?

My friend Linda saw her stint in the hospital as a chance to speak words of faith to the doctors, nurses, and technicians who cared for her.

Jan said her twenty-five-week regimen of radiation gave her twenty-five opportunities to share hope and truth with the patients receiving care alongside her.

At first Susie chafed at the illness that kept her housebound. Then she realized it gave her ample time to pray for others and send notes of spiritual encouragement.

Rachel has a physical limitation that requires her to do life a little differently than most of the world. She leverages her "disability" as an open door to share with others the tips, tricks, and life hacks she's learned along the way.

For years Mary suffered from an emotional wound that brought much hurt into her life. Now she shares her experience with those who have been similarly hurt and offers the comfort and spiritual perspective she's received from God (2 Corinthians 1:4).

The apostle Paul didn't allow his infirmities to keep him from maximizing every chance God gave him to minister in Jesus's name. My friend Mike doesn't either.

As he concluded yet another well-presented and deeply powerful Sunday school lesson, a class member raised her hand. With tears in her eyes, she said, "Mike, you're blind, but you see more than most sighted people ever see. I wish I were more like you."

I'm thankful for people like Paul, Mike, and other friends with physical or emotional struggles. They teach us to embrace every challenge we face as an opportunity, not an **infirmity**.

power

I pray that the eyes of your heart may be enlightened in order that
you may know the hope to which he has called you, the riches of
his glorious inheritance in his holy people, and his incomparably
great power for us who believe. That power is the same as the
mighty strength he exerted when he raised Christ from the dead
and seated him at his right hand in the heavenly realms.

Ephesians 1:18–20

By the time he was seventeen years old, my husband, David, was an
alcoholic and a drug user.

In the years that followed his parents' divorce, he bounced from
one parent to the other, one home to the other, and one state to the
other. A chubby kid with a soft spot for the underdog, he struggled
to fit in.

When adolescence coincided with yet another move, his desire to
find a place to belong, to have someone—anyone—like him moved
him to desperation.

The brainy kids didn't welcome him. He didn't click with the athletes either. But the alcohol and drug crowd greeted him with open, needle-pierced arms. United by a desire to share the next beer, the next joint, the next high, the teens offered friendship and cama-raderie, sucking David into an ever-deepening spiral of addiction.

As he and his friends experimented with new drug combinations, always chasing a higher high, the results became more and more frightening. One night, after downing a particularly dangerous combination of pills and alcohol, David saw and felt things he'd never experienced before. Terrifying images of demons and fright-ening glimpses of otherworldly figures caused him to wonder if he would die that night. If he did, he knew he'd go straight to hell.

"God, help me!" he cried. "I can't quit." He lost consciousness and didn't awaken until morning.

The next day, with his terrifying experience only a memory, he and four friends sat on a brick wall in their neighborhood planning their next high. A tiny woman with a huge smile approached them.

"Hey guys, I'm selling World Book encyclopedias. Do you know where any families with kids live?" They pointed to a house down the road, and she walked away.

Then she turned back.

"I feel led of the Lord to speak to you guys.

"Six months ago my husband and I were using drugs and alcohol. Our marriage was falling apart. He was packing his bags to leave when someone knocked on the door. This man from the church shared with us how Christ had changed his life. He said Jesus could do the same for us.

"When we prayed to receive Christ as our Savior," she said, "God began to change us. He took away our desire for drugs and alcohol. Now I drink as much as I want to—but I don't want to."

When Jolene said the words, "God began to change us," memo-ries from the night before flashed across David's mind. "God," he'd cried, "I want to change, but I can't do it by myself." He realized the God of the universe had heard and answered his prayer.

With Jolene guiding him, he prayed to surrender his life to Christ. "I'm sorry for the things I've done," he said. "I don't want to live like this anymore. I believe you died and rose again to pay for my sins. Change me and make me a new person."

Over time, as God filled him with a desire to find joy in his relationship with Christ, David found strength to refuse the drugs and alcohol. His mentor shared the essence of Ephesians 1:19–20 with him. "The same power that raised Christ from the dead will give you the power to say no to false comforts and destructive behavior."

David filled his mind and heart with God's Word and began to walk in the transformational power God supplied. Every day he surrendered himself to God, confessing, repenting, and receiving the forgiveness God freely offered. His desire for drugs and alcohol lessened and a desire to live in ways that reflected his new allegiance to God grew. Ephesians 3:20–21 describes the miraculous transformation that took place:

"Now to him who is able to do immeasurably more than all we ask or imagine, according to his power that is at work within us, to him be glory in the church and in Christ Jesus throughout all generations, for ever and ever!"

No longer a slave to alcohol, drugs, or fear, David has spent the last forty years growing and becoming more like Christ. He attended a Christian college, surrendered his life to the ministry, and now pastors a church. Ever mindful of how close he came to dying and spending eternity separated from God, he tells everyone who will listen the good news: The same power that raised Christ Jesus from the dead can break the stranglehold of your addiction if you'll surrender your life to Him.

If you or someone you love is drowning in their sin and feels powerless to change, remember this: Within ourselves, we are hopeless. With God, we have resurrection **power**.

think

Finally, brothers and sisters, whatever is true,
whatever is noble, whatever is right, whatever is pure,
whatever is lovely, whatever is admirable—if anything
is excellent or praiseworthy—think about such things.

Philippians 4:8

In the years before I met Christ, my thoughts governed my life. Like a capricious jailer, the voices in my head held the power to hold me captive or set me free. On good days I could accomplish anything, empowered by what I imagined, hoped for, and dreamed of. On bad days my thoughts kept me shackled to the earth by doubts and fears.

Some days I'd break out of my self-defeating prison, buoyed by positive self-talk or a friend's encouragement. But these moments of victory never lasted. All it took was a moment of insecurity or a critical word to upend the delicate balance and send me back to jail again.

When I surrendered my life to Christ, He began to change everything about me, including my thoughts. I learned that instead of being their victim, I had the ability, through Christ, to overpower them. To control them. To shine the light of truth into the dark corners of my mind and expose the lies that held me prisoner.

Second Corinthians 10:5 challenged me to take every thought captive and make it obedient to Christ. Philippians 4:8 showed me how to do it.

"Finally, brothers and sisters, whatever is true, whatever is noble, whatever is right, whatever is pure, whatever is lovely, whatever is admirable—if anything is excellent or praiseworthy—*think about such things*" (emphasis mine).

Paul's challenge to the Philippian believers taught me how to wrestle my thoughts into subjection and make them work *for* me, not against me.

When I applied Philippians 4:8 to filter every thought that raced across my mind, I was able to bring my mind under God's control.

When I feared for the future, truth told me, "So do not fear, for I am with you; do not be dismayed, for I am your God. I will strengthen you and help you; I will uphold you with my righteous right hand" (Isaiah 41:10).

When I felt tempted to lie to protect myself, right thinking encouraged me, "Whoever walks in integrity walks securely" (Proverbs 10:9).

When a lustful thought raced across my mind, pure thinking reminded me, "Flee from sexual immorality" (1 Corinthians 6:18).

As I applied Philippians 4:8 to my internal conversations, my thoughts became sounder and healthier.

I'd like to say this process was one and done for me. Instead it's been a lifelong and never-ending discipline. Some days I slip back into my old way of thinking and allow myself to be paralyzed by fear, anger, or hopelessness. But when I apply the training of Philippians 4:8, I build spiritual muscle memory. I recognize my faulty reasoning sooner and take steps to correct it. I learn to recognize the sound of falsehood's lying footsteps before it ambushes me.

When we surrender our lives to Christ, God calls us to "be transformed by the renewing of your mind" (Romans 12:2). I'm thankful He's given us Scripture like Philippians 4:8 to help us reclaim not only the way we live, but the way we **think**.

wrestling

Epaphras, who is one of you and a servant of Christ Jesus, sends greetings. He is always wrestling in prayer for you, that you may stand firm in all the will of God, mature and fully assured.

Colossians 4:12

When my husband, David, came to Christ, he was so excited about his newfound faith that he shared it with everyone. Unfortunately, he had what the Bible calls zeal without knowledge. Before he knew Christ, he'd communicated with his fists, addressing problems and persuading people using his brawn, not his brains. After he came to faith, he learned more effective and socially acceptable ways to share his perspective.

Except for the time he chased down a friend, pinned him to the ground, and shared the gospel.

"I knew if I held him still long enough to hear the plan of salvation, surely he'd want to pray to accept Christ as his Savior," David said. "And he did. But I think he prayed the prayer just so I'd let him up off the ground."

His brother Luther was bigger than he, so David shared his faith through words. He quoted the Bible verses he'd memorized, shared points from a sermon he heard, or described how God had changed him from an alcoholic drug user to a straight A student headed for Bible college.

After a year of David's relentless witnessing, Luther had had enough.

"If you say one more word to me about Jesus, I'll punch you in the face."

That's when David began to pray more than talk. Where before he had wrestled people to the ground to share his faith with them, he learned to wrestle in prayer, asking that God would open Luther's heart to receive the good news of the gospel.

If David had met Epaphras, a disciple of the apostle Paul, they'd have liked each other. Epaphras also knew how to wrestle in prayer. Bible scholars point to him as the founder of the church of Colossae. Passionate about his congregation and committed to training his people in sound doctrine and godly living, Epaphras labored in prayer for his beloved flock. Paul describes his shepherd's heart in Colossians 4:12: "He is always wrestling in prayer for you, that you may stand firm in all the will of God, mature and fully assured."

The word *wrestle* is a sweaty, gritty word in the original Greek. It appears in several places in the New Testament to describe athletes contending in gymnastic games and people fighting with adversaries. Other times it describes a person struggling with difficulties and dangers from those antagonistic to the gospel.

In Colossians 4:12, however, it describes praying with a strenuous zeal. This is how Epaphras prayed for his congregation. And this is how David prayed for Luther—for twenty-six years.

When Luther joined the army, David prayed. When he moved a thousand miles away, David prayed. When his home caught fire and burned to the ground, David prayed. When his marriage disintegrated, David prayed.

When Luther was diagnosed with cancer, David prayed. He asked God to soften Luther's heart and give him one more chance to share the gospel (without getting punched in the face).

Shortly after Luther's diagnosis, David called his brother. "I heard the news. I'd like to come by and talk with you about your salvation."

"I want to hear what you have to say," Luther replied.

David's years of praying and a life-threatening diagnosis had softened the ground of Luther's heart enough to receive the seeds of the gospel. He listened to David's words and weighed them against the transformation he'd witnessed in his little brother's life.

A week after their conversation, Luther called David. "I thought about what you said." He paused. The angst of twenty-six years squeezed David's chest so tightly it took his breath away. "I prayed and asked Christ to be my Savior."

David's breath escaped his lungs, and silent tears poured down his face. "Congratulations, brother," he said in a voice thick with emotion. "Now you're not only my brother, you're my brother in Christ."

Luther lived four more years after he placed his faith in Jesus. He ended his relationship with his live-in girlfriend, started attending church, and became the most faithful member of our Sunday school class. He read through the Bible for the first time and shared his thoughts with a men's Bible study.

One day he came to me for help.

"I have to write down my testimony for homework. I'm not very good with words. Would you help me?"

I agreed, but he didn't need my help. His words flowed with simple sincerity.

I thought about Christ and how lost I had become. I saw no purpose in my life of loneliness. In my heart I had fear and guilt. I didn't know if God still loved me and would forgive me. Then I remembered John 3:16.

Now that I have a relationship with Christ, I'm not always perfect, but I know God loves me and has a purpose for me. I've found that no matter how bad it gets in my life, I'm not alone as long as I have Jesus to lean on.

Epaphras wrestled in prayer for his beloved congregation. David wrestled in prayer for his big brother. Who are you praying for today?

Don't give up. That breakthrough you've been hoping for could be right around the corner.

Dig in. Pray hard. Keep **wrestling**.

joy

For what is our hope, our joy, or the crown in which we will glory in the presence of our Lord Jesus when he comes? Is it not you?
1 Thessalonians 2:19

Our staff knew Amy would be a great fit for the dental office where I worked. Her resume was stellar. She'd worked as a dental hygienist for twelve years in every city where her husband's job had taken them. She'd even temped for a periodontist, adding specialized training to her list of qualifications.

What impressed us most, however, was her smile. Bright and contagious, Amy's dimpled grin reassured the most anxious patient. Within minutes she'd have them laughing. By the end of their appointment, instead of rushing out as soon as the dentist released them, they'd linger to swap one last story.

I knew something was wrong the day she came to work without her characteristic smile. Marital challenges, the strain of parenting two teenagers, and an upcoming move (their sixth in twelve years) had stolen her happiness.

"I have no peace," she admitted when we talked at lunch. "I'm clueless about how to parent my kids. My marriage is struggling. And I'm afraid—all the time—about what the future holds." Her deep blue eyes shimmered with tears. "I don't know what to do."

"The future can be scary," I agreed. "And when the hard things in life—husbands, teenagers, big decisions—overwhelm us, we feel helpless. This is why we need someone bigger than we are to carry these burdens."

At Amy's nod, I continued. "I've always been a fearful person, but I reached a crisis point when I was eighteen years old. I had decisions to make that would affect the rest of my life, and I was terrified I'd make the wrong choices. I'd been living independent of God, and things weren't turning out as I hoped. I felt very alone." Amy nodded again.

"I spoke to my pastor, and he shared with me what it meant to surrender my life to God and let Him take control." I paused as unexpected tears sprang to my eyes. Leaning forward, I met her gaze. "What he shared with me that day changed my life forever. I still struggle with fear and making decisions, but now I know I'm not alone. The one who controls the world is with me always."

She raised her eyes to meet mine when I asked, "Would you like to hear what my pastor shared with me from the Bible?"

"Yes, I would."

Amy listened carefully. When I finished, she said, "You've given me a lot to think about. Thanks for sharing your story."

The next day at lunch, she told me she had prayed and surrendered her life to Christ.

Although Amy's circumstances didn't change, she did. A hopeful light replaced the frightened one in her eyes. And her always-beautiful smile grew even more beautiful.

Soon her husband's job transferred her away. We communicated by email, but one day my message bounced. As time went on with no word from her, I grew anxious. Was she okay? Was she still walking with the Lord?

In some ways, I felt like the apostle Paul, writing his first letter to the Thessalonians. Concerned for the fledgling church he'd been forced to leave before he'd discipled them, he worried that their faith would flounder.

He loved them as their spiritual father. He'd poured spiritual milk into their hungry mouths as quickly as they could receive it. When persecution required him to flee, he feared they'd get sucked back into their pagan ways.

"When we could stand it no longer, we thought it best to be left by ourselves in Athens. We sent Timothy, who is our brother and co-worker in God's service in spreading the gospel of Christ, to strengthen and encourage you in your faith" (1 Thessalonians 3:1–2).

One day, almost five years after Amy moved away, she showed up in our office. "I'm in town visiting family," she said, "and I had to come by and see you all." We hugged, shared pictures of our kids, and caught up on each other's lives. "I want you to know," she said, "that I meant the prayer I prayed that night. And it's made a difference in my life. Thank you for sharing your faith with me."

My heart soared. I hugged her and blinked back happy tears.

Paul experienced a similar joy. "But Timothy has just now come to us from you and has brought good news about your faith and love. He has told us that you always have pleasant memories of us and that you long to see us, just as we also long to see you" (v. 6).

For Christians, the greatest joy and deepest satisfaction comes from sharing our faith with others and watching God work. The Thessalonians not only stood firm despite persecution, they became home base for the spread of the gospel in Macedonia and Greece.

As Paul told the Thessalonians, "We were encouraged about you because of your faith. For now we really live, since you are standing firm in the Lord" (vv. 7–8).

Unlike the money, fame, or professional success that often accompany the temporary work we do on this earth, the rewards we reap from the spiritual work we do are usually less tangible. But they are infinitely rich. When those we invest in spiritually grow, blossom, and bear fruit, we share God's deep satisfaction and indescribable **joy**.

weary

Do not grow weary in doing good.

2 Thessalonians 3:13 ESV

If you asked Jonelle to describe herself in one word, she'd say, "Weary."

Sarah would too. And Dani. All three are godly Christian women, but they're struggling under challenging circumstances.

Jonelle is married to a difficult man. He's not interested in spiritual things, and he's moody, selfish, and angry. Jonelle is committed to loving and respecting him. She hopes God will use her Christlike love to draw him into a saving relationship with himself. But it's hard. And she grows tired.

Sarah has three young children and a husband who travels a lot. With little time for herself and the constant demands of motherhood, some days she wishes she could run away and never come back. Every time she yells at the kids or resents her husband's travels, she feels like a failure. She loves her family, but she's exhausted.

Dani's daughter Kelsey is wearing her parents out. She's been a handful since she was old enough to chew the lamp cord. Her rebellious spirit often leads her down foolish and self-destructive paths, but now that she's a young adult, the consequences are much more serious. Dani struggles to know the difference between equipping and enabling her daughter. The strain affects every aspect of her life, including her marriage. Dani feels weary.

The Thessalonians were weary too. Persecuted for their faith, battling false teachers, and struggling with doubts and fears, their resolve threatened to crumble. Paul knew this when he wrote, "Do not grow weary in doing good" (2 Thessalonians 3:13 ESV).

Concerned for the baby church he had planted and poured life into, he encouraged them to persevere. A year before he had challenged them, "Rejoice always, pray continually, give thanks in all circumstances; for this is God's will for you in Christ Jesus" (1 Thessalonians 5:16–18).

Now he wrote again to bolster their spirits. "So then, brothers and sisters, stand firm and hold fast to the teachings we passed on to you, whether by word of mouth or by letter" (2 Thessalonians 2:15). Remember what I told you: Rejoice always, even when it's hard. Never stop praying. Give thanks even when you don't feel like it. If you do these things, you'll walk in God's power and not your own. This will enable you to press on, even when you're weary and want to quit.

Paul's words carried weight with the Thessalonians. They'd heard the stories of his imprisonment in Philippi (Acts 16:16–34). Perhaps they'd seen the scars from the beatings he'd received for freeing the slave girl. They might have learned the songs of praise and thanksgiving he and Silas had sung that night in jail.

For certain they knew that the jailer and his whole household had come to faith—because Paul and Silas had pushed past fear and chose to praise God instead. "About midnight," Acts 16:25 tells us,

"Paul and Silas were praying and singing hymns to God, and the prisoners were listening to them."

The Thessalonians were struggling under the load of persecution, faithful Christian service, and love for those God had placed in their lives. In many ways, we are too.

Knowing the burdens were too heavy for them to carry alone, Paul encouraged them to surrender them to God. He says the same to us.

"Do not grow weary in doing good. Rejoice. Pray continually. Give thanks." God will walk beside you and lift your burden. He'll send resources when you have none of your own. He'll lend His strength when you are **weary**.

teaching

If anyone teaches otherwise and does not agree to the sound
instruction of our Lord Jesus Christ and to godly teaching,
they are conceited and understand nothing.

1 Timothy 6:3–4

I'd been a Christian for only six months when I encountered the first challenge to my newborn faith. During a student-led Bible study, the leader made a comment about how we should live holy lives so we wouldn't lose our salvation.

Puzzled by this frightening thought, I questioned him afterward. "What do you mean 'lose our salvation'? Isn't eternal life *eternal*?" His response made my head spin and my heart sink.

Driving home that evening, I replayed our conversation in my mind. The leader had asked me, "Why do you believe in eternal security?"

My answer sounded lame even to my ears: "Because that's what my pastor taught me."

"Maybe you should read the Bible for yourself," he said, and gave me several passages to look up.

As a young believer eager to embrace everything spiritual, I was vulnerable. I hadn't studied the Bible much and depended on others' teaching to shape my beliefs.

There's nothing wrong with learning from wise teachers. Timothy, the young preacher shepherding the church at Ephesus, commended his church members for following "my teaching, my way of life, my purpose, faith, patience, love, endurance" (2 Timothy 3:10).

God gave the Bible for preaching and teaching (v. 16), but God also exhorts us to study His Word for ourselves. We should know it so well we can filter everything we hear through God's Word.

The Bereans in Acts 17 did this. "They received the message with great eagerness and examined the Scriptures every day to see if what Paul said was true." When they confirmed the truth of Paul's message, "many of them believed" (vv. 11–12).

These wise seekers provide a model for us to follow.

We, too, must weigh the teaching of others against the infallible Word of God. To do this, we must become so familiar with the Bible that alarm bells ring in our minds when we hear teaching that doesn't agree with it. My Spider-Man-loving friend calls this "spiritual spidey sense." Just as the comic book character possessed an extraordinary ability to sense danger, we can learn to sense spiritual danger from false teaching and false teachers.

My Bible study leader's challenge was a valuable learning experience for me. It prompted me to dig into God's Word for myself rather than rely solely on my pastor's teaching. I learned to use a concordance and other Bible study tools to examine the verses he shared with me in the context in which they were written. I compared them with others on the same subject and with the teachings of the Bible as a whole.

On a matter so crucial to my spiritual life, I didn't take his word, nor did I take my pastor's word. I found the answers in God's Word:

Eternal life is eternal. I did nothing to earn it, and I can do nothing to lose it. I am saved and kept by God's grace alone.

Since my study those many years ago, I've never wavered or wondered. God settled the matter in my heart, and I have rested in confident trust. I've also learned to choose my teachers wisely. Rather than naively accepting all teaching that presents itself as "Christian," I learned to hold the teacher and the teaching to the standard of God's Word.

I'm grateful God gives us preachers and teachers to guide us into truth and show us how to live the Christian life. I'm especially thankful God gives us the Holy Spirit and His Word to be our ultimate teachers and guides. As we invite God to lead us into all truth, He enables us to spot lies, reject falsehood, and embrace the life-changing power of godly **teaching**.

God-breathed

All Scripture is God-breathed.

2 Timothy 3:16

Cabo San Lucas sits at the south end of the Baja peninsula beneath California. Seven hundred and seventy-five miles of mountains, deserts, and volcanoes separate the lush land of Southern California from this oceanfront tourist town. Known for deep sea fishing and luxurious resorts, Cabo exists as a man-made oasis at the edge of a desert wasteland.

Unlike the fertile fields of the mainland, this barren land can't grow crops. Trucks transport food down the long peninsula from California, and ships bring supplies across the Sea of Cortez.

Cabo does have one export, though—glass. Locals melt the desert sand and form it into exquisite bowls, goblets, ornaments, and home decor.

Our missionary friends Carlos and Sandy gave us a tour of one of the glass shops on our first mission trip to Cabo. I'd never seen anyone blow glass before, and I couldn't wait to see it done.

A smiling man with white teeth and dark eyes stepped up to a molten pot of glass. Inserting a metal pipe into the pot, he scooped up a glowing glob. He placed his lips on the opposite end of the pipe and blew gently. Like a soap bubble on the end of a wand, the glass expanded. Another gentle breath rounded out the shape. A final puff stretched it to the perfect size for his purpose.

He rolled it in bits of colored glass, placed it into a glowing furnace, and molded the shape with his tools.

When his creation was complete, he removed his lips from the pipe and presented the colorful orb with a flourish. We celebrated his masterpiece with oohs and aahs.

I thought of that glassblower when I read the third chapter of 2 Timothy. The apostle Paul reminded the young preacher, "All Scripture is God-breathed and is useful for teaching, rebuking, correcting and training in righteousness" (v. 16).

What did Paul mean when he said Scripture is "God-breathed"?

This all-important phrase, *theopneustos*, is made up of two Greek words: *theos* (God) and *pneō* (to breathe).[11] Other translations use the words "inspired by God" to differentiate the Bible from noninspired writings.

As the molten glass was only a glob until the craftsman breathed into it, so are the writings of men nothing apart from God's inspiration. Those who say the Bible is just a collection of stories compiled by ancient men don't understand this important truth.

God used approximately forty different men to write the Bible, but none wrote under their own inspiration. Through the Holy Spirit, God breathed into them the words and truth He wanted them to write. He used their grammar, style, and personality, but the message of each book is all His.

For those who accept this by faith, the Bible becomes a source of salvation. Paul reminded Timothy of this when he said, "From infancy you have known the Holy Scriptures, which are able to make you wise for salvation through faith in Christ Jesus" (v. 15).

He told the believers in Rome, "Faith comes by hearing, and hearing by the word of God" (Romans 10:17 NKJV).

As the glassblower did, God had specific purposes in mind as He breathed His word into the men who wrote the Bible. Prophets, shepherds, and kings penned the Old Testament and described in graphic detail how lost mankind desperately needs a Savior. Fishermen, Pharisees, and physicians wrote the New Testament to reveal who this Savior is—Jesus, the Lamb of God who takes away the sins of the world.

Books have the power to save lives, but only God's book has the power to save souls.

Once we've placed our faith in Christ, the Bible works together with the Holy Spirit and becomes the agent of our transformation. "All Scripture is God-breathed," Paul wrote, "and is useful for teaching, rebuking, correcting and training in righteousness, so that the servant of God may be thoroughly equipped for every good work" (2 Timothy 3:16–17).

As we read God's Word and invite the Holy Spirit to apply it to our lives, we change. The old us with its sinful desires morphs into a new us with God-honoring desires. Step by baby step, we become more like Jesus.

Hebrews 4:12 describes the Bible as "alive and active. Sharper than any double-edged sword, it penetrates even to dividing soul and spirit, joints and marrow; it judges the thoughts and attitudes of the heart." The Spirit and the Word open our eyes to those things that don't please God. They call us to confess wrong actions and attitudes and turn away from them. They create a desire within us to pursue spiritual growth. As we study the Bible in community with other believers, we learn from each other's insights and grow in faith and godliness.

Life transformation occurs as we read and apply God's Word. From the dawn of creation, men and women have based their lives and their eternal destinies on the same truths we are privileged to read today in God's Word.

As the craftsman breathed into the glob of glass, so God has breathed life-giving and life-sustaining power into His Word.

God-inspired. God-empowered. **God-breathed**.

saved

But when the kindness and love of God our Savior appeared,
he saved us, not because of righteous things we had done,
but because of his mercy.

Titus 3:4–5

You have to be prepared for anything when you date (or marry) someone in the ministry.

Before I met my husband, I dated John. John pastored a small church in a small town and drove a conversion van with squeaky shocks and no air-conditioning.

For our first date, John invited me out to dinner after church on Sunday night. He wanted me to visit his church and hear him preach. Then we'd grab a bite to eat.

If you've ever visited a small church, you know there's nowhere to hide. And when you walk in with the young, single pastor, it's impossible to slip in unnoticed.

I'm not sure "unnoticed" was John's plan as he marched me down the center aisle and seated me smack dab in the middle of the second row. Next to a lady with blue hair and her hard-of-hearing husband.

"The preacher's got a girlfriend," she said to her husband in a stage whisper.

"Huh?" her husband replied, cupping his hand to his ear.

"The preacher's got a girlfriend," she repeated a little louder, leaning in to his good ear.

"The preacher's got a GIRLFRIEND?" he bellowed, leaning forward for a better look. "Well it's about time!"

I smiled weakly and prayed for the service to begin so I could blend into the congregation. After the opening song and before the offering, John stepped to the pulpit.

"I have a special guest with me this evening," he said. "I'd like you to get to know her a bit. Lori, would you come up here and share your testimony with the church?"

So much for blending in. I willed my body to rise. A thousand thoughts swirled in my mind as I made the all-too-short walk from the second row to the pulpit. I'd accepted Christ as my Savior two years earlier, but this was the first time anyone had asked me to share my story. And in front of the whole church, no less.

Gripping the lectern, I faced the congregation and smiled a wobbly smile.

"I've heard a lot of testimonies of how people got saved," I said, fear making my voice tremble. "They say, 'God saved me from drinking,' or 'God saved me from drugs.' Well," I paused, "God saved me from hell!"

The hard-of-hearing man in the second row snorted and several others laughed.

"I didn't drink or do drugs. I was a 'good girl.' I studied hard. Obeyed my parents . . . for the most part . . . and didn't run with the wrong crowd. But I was just as lost and in need of a Savior as an alcoholic or a drug user." I took a deep breath. "Salvation isn't as much about where you've been as it is about where you're going. And I was going straight into an eternity without God."

The apostle Paul wrote to Titus and the believers in Crete to remind them of what their lives were like before Christ. "For we ourselves were also once foolish, disobedient, deceived, serving various lusts and pleasures, living in malice and envy, hateful and hating one another" (Titus 3:3). He reminded them of their past actions not to condemn them but to help them realize how much God had transformed them.

Many of us allow our former lives to silence our witness and hinder our usefulness for God. "I could never speak (serve, lead, teach, mentor, minister)," we say, "because of what I did in my former life." Or, like me, God can't use your story to draw people to himself because it isn't dramatic.

Paul knew what we all need to know—that our past doesn't disqualify us to speak for Christ. It qualifies us.

If we lived a sordid life prior to conversion, we can share how lost we were and how deep God was willing to reach down to rescue us. If we lived a squeaky-clean life (notice I didn't say perfect—no one is perfect except Jesus), we can share how "good people" (people who think they're good) also need to be saved.

The same God who saved a wretch like me can save a wretch like you. And make no mistake, we're all wretches (to quote the old hymn). "Good" girls are no more fit for heaven than "bad" ones. We've all sinned and fallen short of God's standard (Romans 3:23).

"He saved us," Paul reminded his readers, "not because of righteous things we had done, but because of his mercy" (Titus 3:5). Good works don't save us. Christ does. Although our pasts may look very different, we share the same message.

Whether your past was sordid or saintly, God can use your story to point people to salvation.

That day in church I joined the ranks of the alcoholics and drug users to testify that our former lives, no matter what they looked like, prove we all need Jesus.

What were you formerly? What are you now?

Will you trust God with your past and allow Him to use it for His purposes? Will you share your story with others? There's someone in your circle of influence who needs to be **saved**.

appeal

*Therefore, although in Christ I could be bold and order you
to do what you ought to do, yet I prefer to appeal
to you on the basis of love.*

Philemon 1:8–9

Pastor Lincoln was a wise man. Although God and the church had granted him authority to make decisions and carry them out, he never led our congregation with a heavy hand. One Sunday evening he called a meeting.

"Our church is growing, and this is a good thing. More people are attending Sunday school and worship, our children's ministry is expanding, and our youth outreach attracts new students every week. Each person who walks through the door hears the gospel and has the opportunity to come to know Christ.

"In order to meet everyone's needs, the deacons and I have decided to add a third service on Sunday morning—just until our new building is completed. The service will begin at 8 a.m." A few groans arose from the congregation.

"This is where you come in. I'd like to ask you, the most faithful, loving, serving members of our church, to attend the early service. I know it will be an inconvenience, but this is the best way to make room for visitors in our second and third services."

That wasn't all. "We're also having a parking problem. Visitors say they come to church but leave because they can't find a parking place. I'd like to ask you, if you're physically able, please park at the far end of our property. This will open up the more convenient spaces for visitors."

"I can't make any of you do this," he admitted. "But I appeal to you for the sake of the church, the people we hope to reach, and the gospel."

I suspect our pastor learned to lead by studying the apostle Paul. Spearheading the greatest evangelistic campaign ever, Paul and his team of ministers brought the gospel to the Gentiles. He wrote more books of the New Testament than any other writer. He planted churches throughout Asia, endured unimaginable cruelty, and suffered persecution for his faith.

He wrote the letter to Philemon from a Roman prison. In God's mysterious providence, Paul and Onesimus, a runaway slave, had crossed paths. Onesimus came to faith in Christ, became a disciple, and helped meet Paul's needs. Both knew Onesimus had a moral obligation, as a Christian, to return to his master.

Paul wrote an impassioned plea to Onesimus's owner, Philemon. He reminded Philemon of their shared history. How Philemon had come to faith in Christ because of Paul's ministry. How they had partnered together. He mentioned his own imprisonment and advancing age.

Then, after Paul listed all the reasons he could rightfully force or compel Philemon to accept Onesimus back without punishment, he wiped the slate clean. He cast aside his iron-clad case and appealed to Philemon on the basis of love.

"Therefore, although in Christ I could be bold and order you to do what you ought to do, yet I prefer to appeal to you on the basis of love. It is as none other than Paul—an old man and now also a prisoner of Christ Jesus—that I appeal to you," he said in Philemon verses 8–9.

"I am sending him—who is my very heart—back to you. I would have liked to keep him with me so that he could take your place in helping me while I am in chains for the gospel. But I did not want to do anything without your consent, so that any favor you do would not seem forced but would be voluntary" (vv. 12–14).

Paul knew love is an infinitely more powerful motivator than guilt, compulsion, or obligation. He also knew forcing someone to do what's right breeds resentment and anger. Appealing to a person's heart of love invites them to set aside their personal rights for the glorious cause of Christ.

Yet Paul didn't end with his appeal. He offered to pay the price for Onesimus's sin. "Put it on my account," he said. "I will repay."

Paul set aside his ability to force someone to comply and chose instead to make a biblical appeal. To trust the Holy Spirit to work. To invite others to do the right thing. When my pastor appealed to our congregation, the members willingly adjusted their worship times and parking spots so visitors could hear the gospel.

Scripture doesn't tell us how Philemon responded to Paul's appeal. Christians don't always choose to do what is right, but a wise leader knows how to give them the opportunity.

We may not be the great apostle Paul or the pastor of a large church, but we can follow their examples.

When we lead with biblical humility, we invite others to experience the joy of responding to a gospel-centered, God-honoring **appeal**.

once

We have been made holy through the sacrifice of the body
of Jesus Christ once for all.

Hebrews 10:10

For years I suffered from a recurring dream.

I'd awaken panicked, my heart racing, and sweat drenching my body. The details of the dream would slip away almost instantly, but it always left me with an overwhelming sense of futility.

Remember the classic chocolate factory episode from the *I Love Lucy* show? Ethel and Lucy were hired to wrap chocolates on an assembly line. At first the pace was manageable, but the bon bons came faster and faster down the conveyor belt until they overwhelmed the pair. Ethel and Lucy stuffed chocolates into their pockets, bodices, and even their mouths in an attempt to keep up. Before long, they were overwhelmed.

You may think an avalanche of chocolate sounds more like a dream come true than a nightmare, but what links this episode with my dream is the profound sense of hopelessness the women felt. It was obvious. If they wrapped chocolate from sun up to sun down, they'd never complete the task.

In a much more serious way, I suspect the Old Testament priests felt this hopelessness as they offered sacrifices for the Israelites' sins in the temple. From sun up to sun down, they watched guilty men and women lay their hands on the heads of animals, admit their sinfulness, and watch as an innocent animal died in their place. The writer of Hebrews described it this way: "Day after day every priest stands and performs his religious duties; again and again he offers the same sacrifices, which can never take away sins" (10:11). Can you imagine being called to a task designed to fail?

Worse yet, imagine being one of the Israelites leaving the temple after offering your sacrifice. Clean for a moment, or maybe an hour, until the next sinful thought, unkind word, or selfish action undid your sacrifice and separated you from God—again.

We don't have to stretch to imagine this, because it describes us, too, before Jesus rescued us. We know, in the deepest part of our heart, that we can never be good enough. We can never do enough good works to outweigh the bad we've done—even if we're a "pretty good" person. "Pretty good" people still fall far short of God's perfect standard.

But glory halleluiah, Jesus, through His death on the cross, made a way.

"When this priest [Jesus] had offered for all time one sacrifice for sins, he sat down at the right hand of God. . . . For by one sacrifice he has made perfect forever those who are being made holy" (vv. 12–14).

The death of Jesus on the cross—the sinless for the sinful—ended the futility of our attempts to be good enough to earn God's favor. It ushered in a new way, a better way. A *once-for-all* way.

> "This is the covenant I will make with them
>   after that time, says the Lord.

I will put my laws in their hearts,
  and I will write them on their minds."

Then he adds:

"Their sins and lawless acts
  I will remember no more."
And where these have been forgiven, sacrifice for
  sin is no longer necessary. (vv. 16–18)

When I placed my faith in Christ, in God's eyes I wasn't merely good enough. I was counted as "perfect" (v. 14). I'll spend the rest of my life growing in holiness and seeking to become more like Christ, but my sin debt is settled. Jesus paid it all.

Several years passed before I realized I hadn't had my recurring dream. When did it stop? When I placed my faith in Christ. Was my dream the expression of my hopeless soul? I don't know. Was it a coincidence that my overwhelming feelings of futility ended when I received Jesus's payment for my sin?

Those who have trusted Christ can come to God, "with a sincere heart and with the full assurance that faith brings, having our hearts sprinkled to cleanse us from a guilty conscience and having our bodies washed with pure water" (v. 22).

If Christ is our Savior, we can "hold unswervingly to the hope we profess, for he [God] who promised is faithful" (v. 23).

Our worst nightmare—a mountain of sins we can never atone for—becomes a distant memory when we trust in Jesus, who paid for all our sin **once**.

doers

Do not merely listen to the word, and so deceive yourselves.
Do what it says.

James 1:22

Every time I read the book of James, I remember the summer of 2012.

My daughter had just completed her freshman year of college and decided to stay in Virginia to work. We talked often, and one day I asked her how her recently graduated boyfriend, Josiah, was doing.

"He's filled out more than a hundred applications," she said, "but he still hasn't found a job. The market is saturated with business majors. He's doing odd jobs to earn money, but I'm worried about him. He's getting pretty skinny."

"I'm so sorry," I said. "Dad and I have been praying for him to find a job. We'll pray harder." We chatted for a few more minutes, then I said goodbye.

As soon as I hung up the phone, I remembered the words from my morning study in the book of James.

"What good is it, my brothers and sisters, if someone claims to have faith but has no deeds? Can such faith save them? Suppose a brother or a sister is without clothes and daily food. If one of you says to them, 'Go in peace; keep warm and well fed,' but does nothing about their physical needs, what good is it? In the same way, faith by itself, if it is not accompanied by action, is dead" (James 2:14–17).

Shame flooded my face as I realized I'd done just what this passage describes—I heard about a legitimate need, slapped on a Band-Aid promise to pray, and moved on.

James 1:22 sealed the deal: "Do not merely listen to the word, and so deceive yourselves. Do what it says."

"Lord," I prayed, "Josiah has a legitimate need, and we have the means to help him. James 1:5 promises, 'If any of you lacks wisdom, you should ask God, who gives generously to all without finding fault, and it will be given to you.' Please show us how to help without embarrassing him, discouraging him, or getting in the way of what you're doing in his life. Amen."

I thought for a bit, then called my husband. I explained the situation and ended with, "I just read the passage in James about not turning your back on a legitimate need, and I was wondering if we could help him. Remember that extra money we wondered what to do with?"

"Absolutely," my generous-hearted husband said, "I'd be glad to help. Mail him a check today."

"I doubt he'll accept money," I said. "He wants to work. Maybe he could paint our house."

"But our house doesn't need painting," David said.

"Yes, it does."

"No, it doesn't. We just had it painted two years ago."

"David, our house needs painting."

"Hmmmm," he said, "now that you mention it, our house *does* need painting. I'll call him today."

Few, if any of us, can help every struggling college student, homeless person, or charity, but we can all obey God's Word. We can all give generously when the means and the opportunity present themselves.

That morning, God reminded me what a privilege it is to bless others with the resources He's entrusted to us. He gave me a chance to put into practice what I had just learned. To be a doer of the Word, not just a hearer.

"We'll pay your gas to and from Virginia," my husband said when he called Josiah. "You're welcome to stay with us. It'll be good to have a young person sitting around the dinner table again."

Within two days Josiah was hard at work on our house. We put out the word to friends and neighbors, and soon he had three more weeks of work lined up. Two days before he finished the last job, he got a call from a shipping company in Virginia offering him a full-time job.

When he drove away, we had a beautifully painted house and the satisfaction of knowing we'd obeyed God's command.

A year later, that hard-working young man became our son-in-law. In time he became the father of our four grandchildren. He continues to work hard and do whatever it takes to provide for his family. And every now and then, he helps us out with a painting project—for old time's sake.

When we offered to help a person in need, we had no idea we were investing in our future son-in-law. We just wanted to obey God's Word.

I'm so glad we chose to be hearers *and* **doers**.

surprised

Dear friends, do not be surprised at the fiery ordeal
that has come on you to test you,
as though something strange were happening to you.

1 Peter 4:12

My childhood dentist was a liar.

"You won't feel a thing," he said as he pointed an eighteen-inch needle at my mouth. Poke. Jab. *Pain!* He must have meant I wouldn't feel a thing *after* the shot, 'cause I sure felt something *during* the shot.

"Ahhhhhhhhhh!" I yelled—loudly enough to clear the waiting room and the parking lot.

I don't know what wounded me more, the prick of the needle or the sting of surprise.

My second dentist took a different approach.

"First you'll feel a pinch," he said. "Then you'll feel a sting. By the time you count to four, you'll begin to feel numb, and it won't hurt anymore."

I opened my mouth.

He raised the needle.

I closed my eyes.

Ouch! One thousand one, one thousand two, one thousand three, one thousand four.

He was right. It did pinch. And it did sting. And it did go away.

Knowing the pinch and the sting were coming helped me respond properly. Because the shot (and its accompanying pain) didn't catch me by surprise, I could prepare myself. I could endure, because I knew it would end. The reward on the other side (a coupon for a free McDonald's ice cream) helped too.

The apostle Peter, writing to first-century Christians, employed the same approach my second dentist used.

His audience, victims of intense harassment by the emperor Nero and his evil henchmen, had fled their homes in Jerusalem. Romans and Jews defamed, slandered, boycotted, mobbed, and imprisoned them. Many lost their homes and businesses. Some lost their lives.

In love with God, committed to each other, and passionate about sharing Christ with those around them, the early believers were shocked by the hatred and abuse directed at them. They'd committed no punishable offense. The only "crime" they'd done was to pledge their allegiance to Christ and live in obedience to His teachings.

Peter, however, wasn't shocked.

"Dear friends," he wrote, "do not be surprised at the fiery ordeal that has come on you to test you, as though something strange were happening to you" (1 Peter 4:12). Peter's matter-of-fact, almost casual acknowledgment of the Christians' suffering wasn't an attempt to minimize their struggles.

Instead, he sought to affirm and encourage them. *Fiery* describes a heat so intense it would burn away impurities in metals. This trial hasn't come to punish you, Peter said to them, but to refine you. It's proof of your faith and commitment to Christ.

Perhaps he'd read Paul's words to Timothy and the church in Ephesus, "Everyone who wants to live a godly life in Christ Jesus will be persecuted" (2 Timothy 3:12).

Or maybe he remembered Jesus's words. "Be on your guard; you will be handed over to the local councils and be flogged in the synagogues. On my account you will be brought before governors and kings as witnesses to them and to the Gentiles. But when they arrest you, do not worry about what to say or how to say it. . . . You will be hated by everyone because of me" (Matthew 10:17–19, 22).

With these predictions swirling in his head, Peter sought to remind the church they would suffer persecution. If they didn't realize and expect it, they'd be caught unprepared—and it would hurt even more.

As did first-century Christians, we must expect persecution. "In this world," Jesus said, "you will have trouble. But take heart! I have overcome the world" (John 16:33).

Today's world is no friend of believers. Cultures grow increasingly anti-Christian. Societies reject the truth of God's Word. Governments restrict Christian liberties. Education mocks faith. Although we in America haven't experienced the degree of persecution our brothers and sisters endure in other parts of the world, we, too, suffer.

When persecution comes, we shouldn't be surprised. Rather, as Peter challenged, "Rejoice inasmuch as you participate in the sufferings of Christ, so that you may be overjoyed when his glory is revealed. If you are insulted because of the name of Christ, you are blessed, for the Spirit of glory and of God rests on you. If you suffer, it should not be as a murderer or thief or any other kind of criminal, or even as a meddler. However, if you suffer as a Christian, do not be ashamed, but praise God that you bear that name" (1 Peter 4:13–16).

Let's accept Peter's charge to view persecution as a blessing and an honor. Praising God in the midst of our trial will remind us that like the long needle my dentist told me was coming, persecution will pinch and sting, but it won't last forever. A future triumph awaits us.

When persecution comes, in small ways or in big, we should expect it. When we do, we're better able to respond like the early believers did—with their eyes on the Savior and their hearts set on their reward. Let's determine today to accept our trials as a crown of identification with Jesus, and praise God for the opportunity to suffer for His name.

Expecting persecution won't take the sting away, but it will help us remember that the pain is temporary. Relief, reward, and rejoicing will come.

Be ready. Don't be **surprised**.

promise

In keeping with his promise we are looking forward to a new
heaven and a new earth, where righteousness dwells.

2 Peter 3:13

Picture a four-year-old child alone in a room with a single marsh-mallow on a plate in front of him. In the now-famous Stanford marshmallow experiment, researchers set a marshmallow in front of four- to six-year-old children and offered them two choices—eat it immediately or wait until the researcher returned. If they waited, they'd receive a second marshmallow. The test was designed to measure a child's ability to delay gratification for a promised future reward.

While the kids waited, they passed the time in a variety of creative ways. One boy raised the marshmallow to his nose, closed his eyes, and inhaled deeply. A little girl with ponytails licked her marshmallow—only once—rubbing her tongue around her mouth to savor every tasty molecule.

Other kids waited more actively. They fidgeted, squirmed, and tugged at their hair. "Some children who waited with both treats in sight would stare at a mirror, cover their eyes, or talk to themselves."[12]

If I participated in the marshmallow experiment, I'd fidget the whole time. Maybe even pound the table once or twice. I don't wait well.

The Christians in the first century AD would have been right there with me. With Jesus's promises to return echoing in their ears, they wondered when He would come back to establish His kingdom and reward His faithful followers. Seventy years had passed, and they were getting antsy. They fidgeted. They stomped. They questioned.

The skeptics around them stirred their angst. "Where is this 'coming' he promised?" they scoffed. "Ever since our ancestors died, everything goes on as it has since the beginning of creation" (2 Peter 3:4).

Now, two thousand years later, we're still waiting for Jesus's return. As the world around us disintegrates, our faith can easily wobble. What if Jesus never returns? What if Christianity and the Bible are, as the skeptics of Peter's day said, "cleverly devised stories" (1:16)? Jesus did come once. What if He was the only marshmallow we get? We'd better gobble what benefit we can, because there may not be a second.

Like the Stanford researchers, Peter encourages us to hang on. He reminds us that a great reward awaits us if we remain steadfast. "Don't doubt Jesus's promises," he says. "I heard God's voice from heaven telling us Jesus was His beloved Son. You can trust Him."

"The Lord is not slow in keeping his promise, as some understand slowness. Instead he is patient with you, not wanting anyone to perish, but everyone to come to repentance" (3:9).

God hasn't been idle these two thousand years. He's been gathering a great harvest of souls and giving everyone an opportunity to place their faith in Christ—to become part of God's family. If Jesus had come back in the first century when scoffers called him a liar and Christians doubted, you and I wouldn't even be here. We would never have existed to experience His goodness. Our children and grandchildren would never have lived and had opportunity to know and worship Him.

Instead, with faithfulness and longsuffering, God has given us and untold numbers of people the chance to glimpse Him in creation, hear about Him from others, and learn about Him through His Word. Then, when the fullness of time has come and the last soul has accepted Him as Savior, we'll receive something far greater than a second marshmallow. We'll receive a life more delicious than anything we could ever hope for or imagine.

"In keeping with his promise we are looking forward to a new heaven and a new earth, where righteousness dwells" (v. 13). No sickness. No pain. No sorrow. No tears. Just a blissful eternity with God and those who love Him.

"So then, dear friends, since you are looking forward to this, make every effort to be found spotless, blameless and at peace with him. Bear in mind that our Lord's patience means salvation" (vv. 14–15).

When we're tempted to doubt, give up, or give in to the world's methods and philosophies, we can stand firm, knowing we can trust God's **promise**.

in

The one who is in you is greater than the one who is in the world.

1 John 4:4

When my daughter was almost three, we discovered we were expecting another baby. As my belly grew, I had a hard time keeping up with my energetic toddler.

One day as I sprinted (waddled) across the playground in an attempt to catch her, a friend commented, "Imagine chasing two around. At least for a while, your second one goes everywhere you go."

I thought about her insightful comment when I read the letter of 1 John. Written to Gentile believers, this book contains hopeful and empowering words. One of my favorite verses, 1 John 4:4, parts the curtain on a precious fact about the relationship between the Holy Spirit and the believer.

"The one who is in you is greater than the one who is in the world."

Did you catch that teeny tiny two-letter word that makes all the difference?

In.

In Old Testament days, the Holy Spirit, the third Person of the Godhead, acted in much the same way as He does today. He inspired believers (Isaiah 6:8), empowered them (Numbers 27:18), and spoke through them (Ezekiel 2:2).

But He also left them.

When a believer resisted His leadership and willfully and continuously sinned, God removed the Holy Spirit's presence from their life. You can read King's Saul's story in 1 Samuel 16 for an example of this.

But something changed between the Old and New Testaments. God replaced the old covenant with the new. Instead of being motivated by the external law, God-followers would be motivated by an internally changed heart. The power behind this changed heart would be the indwelling Holy Spirit. Listen to Ezekiel's prophecy:

"I will put my Spirit in you and move you to follow my decrees and be careful to keep my laws" (Ezekiel 36:27).

Did you catch that? God said, "I will put my Spirit *in* you." No longer would the power and presence of the Holy Spirit come and go. He lives in believers forever.

The apostle Paul told the Christians at Ephesus, "When you believed, you were marked in him with a seal, the promised Holy Spirit, who is a deposit guaranteeing our inheritance until the redemption of those who are God's possession" (Ephesians 1:13–14).

Paul mentioned how the Holy Spirit assures us of our salvation and God's presence during times of doubt and trial. "The Spirit himself testifies with our spirit that we are God's children" (Romans 8:16). Deep down in our souls, the Holy Spirit gives us a knowing. Though our sin can damage our fellowship with God, our relationship remains unchanged. He has sealed us as His own forever. Our heavenly Father will never unadopt us or remove His Spirit from us. The Holy Spirit guarantees our salvation.

John, in the first of three letters, reminded us of the unlimited power at work within us through the indwelling Holy Spirit. "The one who is in you is greater than the one who is in the world" (1 John 4:4). He affirmed what Paul taught, that the same power that raised Christ Jesus from the dead makes its home in us (Romans 8:11), enabling us to live victoriously in this challenging world.

Christians often say they're "charging hell with a squirt gun." Instead, through the power of the Holy Spirit living in us, we possess the ability to resist sin's influence, destroy the works of the devil, and positively impact the world around us.

The Holy Spirit's power in us is wider, deeper, stronger, and more victorious than anything the devil possesses. God's grace, through the transformational work of the Holy Spirit, "teaches us to say 'No'" to the sinful way we used to live and choose instead to "live self-controlled, upright and godly lives" (Titus 2:12). Best of all, the Holy Spirit gives us power to fight against the spiritual forces of evil that attempt to destroy us and those we love (Ephesians 6:12).

That unsaved loved one you're praying for? The addiction you're battling? The secret sin that keeps you defeated? The culture that seems to be destroying everything we love about our world? God *in* us, in the Person of the Holy Spirit, is greater than any of these. We are not powerless. We are powerful.

Because of this truth, we don't lose heart. We persevere when we want to quit. We press on when we feel like failures. We stay the course when the journey is long.

That little one I carried within my body and under my heart went everywhere I went for nine months. God, in the person of the Holy Spirit, is with me forever.

I'm so thankful Scripture reminds us that God the Holy Spirit is not just *with* believers, He is **in**

truth

Grace, mercy and peace from God the Father and from Jesus Christ, the Father's Son, will be with us in truth and love.

2 John 1:3

"I've been concerned for quite a while," Lily, a young woman from my church, said. "I don't know what to do."

Tenderhearted Lily often sought my input as she learned to navigate the Christian life. That day I could tell she was particularly troubled.

Her friend Chelsea, who'd walked closely with the Lord, was wandering from the faith. "Usually, she makes decisions based on the Bible," Lily said, "but now she's 'following her heart.'" She wiggled her fingers in air quotes, "and 'listening to her inner voice.'"

Not surprisingly, her heart and her inner voice were leading her down dangerous paths. Her sin didn't allow her to follow God.

"What should I do?" Lily asked. "I have to say something. She's my friend. I can't pretend I don't see the choices she's making." She drew a deep breath, and tears sprang to her eyes. "I'm afraid it will damage our friendship if I say something. But God's Word tells us to speak the truth to those who are wandering" (James 5:19–20).

"Let's pray and ask God for wisdom," I said. As we talked more, she knew God was calling her to speak the truth in love.

The apostle John addressed the letter of 2 John to "the lady chosen by God and to her children, whom I love in the truth" (2 John 1:1).

Again and again, he wove the twin threads of God's heart through the four books that bear his name: Love and truth. Truth and love. These shining strands define how we relate to God and chart the course for every interaction we have with others. Like guardrails on a mountain road, they guide and protect us.

"God is Spirit," John declared, "and his worshipers must worship in the Spirit *and in truth*" (John 4:24).

The Bible defines truth as the doctrine that comes from God—every word the Bible contains, not just the parts we like. The blessings and the curses. The verses that make us feel good ("Never will I leave you; never will I forsake you," Hebrews 13:5) and the verses that warn us away from dangerous behavior ("You shall not . . . ," Exodus 20).

This contradicts today's culture, which declares there is no absolute or moral truth. That everyone is free to set their own moral compass and live by their own rules. Although this often presents itself as a new, enlightened, modern philosophy, it's not. Pontius Pilate hinted at a similar mindset when he asked Jesus, "What is truth?" (John 18:38).

If he'd done his research, he'd have known Jesus had already answered his question when he said. "I am the way and the truth and the life. No one comes to the Father except through me" (14:6).

Even as a new believer, Lily knew she needed to love her friend by speaking the truth. She understood that love sometimes requires us to say and do hard things and risk a temporary rift to bring about a lasting reconciliation.

When I shared John's promise to the church, a peace settled over her. "Grace, mercy and peace from God the Father and from Jesus Christ, the Father's Son, will be with us *in truth and love*" (2 John 1:3).

Lily asked God for the right opportunity to talk with Chelsea. When it came, she reminded her of how much she valued their friendship. Then she shared biblical truth. "I want God's best for you, and the path you're traveling isn't it."

I wish I could say Chelsea received Lily's words in the spirit in which they were spoken. That she realized the truth and altered her path. I'd love to tie up their story with a big red bow and declare that they all lived happily ever after, but I can't. Not yet.

Lily continues to pray for Chelsea. She seeks ways to minister to her. When God gives her an opportunity, she speaks the truth—in love.

She hopes one day soon to be able to experience "the great joy" the apostle John felt when he learned his loved ones were "walking in the **truth**" (2 John 1:4).

face

I have much to write you, but I do not want to do so with pen and ink. I hope to see you soon, and we will talk face to face.

3 John 1:13–14

My husband, David, and I met when he was home from college on Christmas break. I was completing my final year in dental hygiene school in Columbia, South Carolina, and he was midway through his junior year at Liberty Baptist College (now Liberty University) in Lynchburg, Virginia. We liked each other instantly and spent as much time together as possible. Then he returned to Virginia, and I stayed in Columbia to prepare for national boards and graduation.

We dated long before cell phones and computers allowed people to see and talk to each other in real time. The only phone available to him was a pay phone in the dormitory hall that gobbled quarters as fast as a kid eating jelly beans. Needless to say, we didn't talk often.

But every night for the better part of a year, I wrote him a letter. I was so smitten I couldn't bear to fall asleep without telling him about my day, reminding him I was praying for him, and expressing my love. When he returned from college, he brought home an impressive stack of mail smelling faintly of my perfume. (Yes, I actually did this.)

"I love your letters," he told me. "I can't wait to go to my mailbox every day and find one waiting for me."

My stack of love notes from David contained a birthday card, a Valentine's card, and four thin envelopes with his dorm room address hastily scribbled in the left-hand corner.

"It's not that I don't want to respond to your letters," David explained. "I'm just not a writer. I'd rather see your face and talk to you in person."

He proved it.

Official policy prohibited students from leaving campus more than twice a semester, but David somehow managed to wheedle, cajole, and connive ways to come home—often.

His Plymouth Champ was so old only two out of its four cylinders fired, but somehow he made it home and back, sputtering up and down the mountains of Virginia more times than I could count.

John—the writer of the New Testament letters of 1, 2, and 3 John—and David have a lot in common. John's letters were also short and scarce. His letter to his beloved friend Gaius is the shortest book in the Bible. A featherweight weighing in at 219 words, 3 John is even shorter than his previous letter, 2 John, which tips the scales at 245 words.

In this short epistle, John expressed his love and admiration for Gaius. He encouraged him in the faith and challenged him to continue in good works. Then he concluded with these words (which made he and David best friends): "I have much to write you, but I do not want to do so with pen and ink. I hope to see you soon, and we will talk face to face."

Face to face. Can you think of a time when you desperately yearned to see someone you loved face to face? To look into their eyes? To watch their face light up? To wrap your arms around them and squeeze them so hard they can't breathe?

I'm grateful for technology that lets us compose and send text messages in seconds, shoot an email around the world, and see each other in real time on our devices. But these methods are, at best, only adequate when it comes to communicating. There's nothing like spending time together in the same room, laughing, crying, and enjoying each other's company.

Time and distance often prevent this, but not always. Sometimes we allow busyness (or laziness) to keep us apart. It takes effort to meet someone for lunch, have friends over for dinner, or grab coffee together. It's easier to slide by with an occasional *How are you doing?* text than carve out the time and energy to get together in person.

But oh, when we do, how the conversation flows. How our hearts open, our spirits lift, and our love grows. "As iron sharpens iron," Proverbs 27:17 reminds us, "so one person sharpens another." The writer of Proverbs 11:25 agrees, "A generous person will prosper; whoever refreshes others will be refreshed."

Realizing how the tyranny of the urgent can crowd out our time with friends and family, David and I set a goal to invite someone to our home or out to dinner at least once a month. We set additional goals to each ask a friend or friends to meet us for lunch once a month. These goals are small but doable. At the beginning of each month, we plan who we'll invite and then reach out. By the end of the year, we'll have enjoyed thirty-six in-person get togethers. Wow!

How long has it been since you've seen a friend or loved one in person? Why not reach out today and set a date to get together?

I'm thankful for modern technology so I can connect with loved ones far away. Letters, texts, and phone calls have their place in the ebb and flow of our relationships, but it should never replace spending time together under the same roof. Technology will do in a pinch, but as David and John agree, there's nothing better than seeing one another face to **face**.

contend

Dear friends, although I was very eager to write to you
about the salvation we share, I felt compelled to write
and urge you to contend for the faith that was once
for all entrusted to God's holy people.

Jude 1:3

"We're leaving our church," Kayla told me one afternoon.

"What?" I said. "What do you mean, you're leaving your church? You and Curt are founding members. He's a deacon. You lead the women's ministry. How can you leave your church?"

"We've been concerned about the direction the church has been going in for several years now," Kayla said. "But about a year ago, one of the deacons attended a conference that introduced some questionable doctrine. He brought it back to the church. Now even the pastor's teaching it."

Her voice rose in frustration. "We met with the guy several times to share our concerns. He got all defensive and offended. When he wouldn't listen, we met with the pastor. We finally shared our concerns with the entire leadership team."

She fiddled with her napkin, twisted it into a knot, then lifted tear-filled eyes to meet mine. "Even though we showed them from the Bible how their teaching is clearly wrong, they wouldn't listen." She took a deep breath and let out a long sigh. "We have no choice but to leave. We can't continue to associate ourselves with a church whose teaching contradicts the Bible."

Kayla is a peacemaking people-pleaser who loves nothing more than for everyone to get along. She'll give up her seat, her ticket, or her last piece of chocolate to minimize conflicts. When she and her husband became aware of the doctrinal issues creeping into their beloved church, they were tempted to ignore them. They loved the people. They'd poured twenty years of their lives into the ministry. They'd invested money in its outreach.

But they knew they had to be true to God's Word. They couldn't compromise. They had to defend the faith.

As they prayed for wisdom, they found it in the tiny New Testament book of Jude. The brother of James and the half brother of Jesus, Jude was a respected leader in the early church. Like Kayla and Curt, he preferred to talk and write about the happier side of church life.

He loved telling fellow believers how the gospel was advancing and how many people had accepted Christ as their Savior in his church. About spiritual victories and answers to prayer. About the joy of walking with Christ.

But he had a very different purpose for writing the letter that bears his name. "Dear friends, although I was very eager to write to you about the salvation we share, I felt compelled to write and urge you to contend for the faith that was once for all entrusted to God's holy people" (v. 3).

In the years after Christ's death and resurrection, many false teachers sprang up. The canon of Scripture was incomplete, so believers in the early churches didn't have a way to fact check. Although the apostles did their best to share what they'd learned from Jesus, they couldn't be everywhere at once. They traveled from church to church teaching and appointing leaders who would uphold the truth. When they couldn't visit physically, they wrote letters that circulated among the churches to clarify issues and untangle theological knots.

When Jude heard false teachers had infiltrated his beloved church, he took out his parchment and pen. Under the inspiration of the Holy Spirit, he exposed the false teachers and their motives. "They are ungodly people, who pervert the grace of our God into a license for immorality and deny Jesus Christ our only Sovereign and Lord" (v. 4). He reminded them of the true gospel that had transformed their lives. He exhorted them to zealously fight for the faith.

Today we have excellent translations of the Bible to help us evaluate every teaching that comes our way. But our Bibles won't help us unless we know them well enough to spot falsehood and false teachers. Online resources from theologically sound sources also provide ways to compare teaching with biblical truth.[13]

It's not enough to know the truth and live by it. As Jude exhorted, we must *contend* for the faith. Defend God's Word when it's misrepresented. Share truth when the opportunity presents itself. Expose false teaching and false teachers.

Jesus warned his disciples, "For false messiahs and false prophets will appear and perform great signs and wonders to deceive, if possible, even the elect" (Matthew 24:24). We must not be surprised by this. We must be ready.

Like Jude (and Kayla), I prefer to focus on the happy parts of the Christian life. But to be true to the faith God entrusted to His children, I must be willing to **contend**.

new

My husband, David, grew up taking family vacations at the beach. Every summer his parents rented a camper at PirateLand in Myrtle Beach, South Carolina. They'd spend the week enjoying the sun, seashore, and sky; eating hot dogs and drinking Kool-Aid. Like his favorite pair of shorts, summer vacation at the beach was comfortable and familiar.

This is why, when one of his mission teammates suggested they take the boys from their summer Bible study to the beach, David said, "What if we took them to a baseball game instead, or to the go-kart track? Let's do something they've never done before."

South Central Los Angeles, where he and his fellow students from Bible college were serving, was only thirty minutes from the beach. Surely it couldn't have much of a wow factor.

Greg, the team leader disagreed. "I bet none of these kids have ever been to the beach. All they know is concrete, traffic, and graffiti."

Sure enough, when they proposed the idea to the students the next day, Greg was right.

"You wanna take us to the ocean?" Chris, a lanky twelve-year-old, said, sitting up straight. "I've been askin' my mama all my life to take us, but we don't have a car, and the bus doesn't go there."

"Will there be waves and sea gulls and fish?" Chris's younger brother, Gene, asked. He talked so fast his words tumbled over themselves. "Can I wear my bathing suit? And hunt for seashells? And swim—except I don't know how to swim—but you can teach me."

So off they went, six kids and six college students, down I-120 to Redondo Beach. As Greg turned into the parking lot, he yelled over the excited chatter that filled the van.

"Hey kids, close your eyes. And no peeking!"

Each student took a boy by the arm and led him across the parking lot to the sandy shore. They pointed the boys in the direction of the sea.

"Okay," Greg said. "Open your eyes."

At first the boys stared, their eyes wide and darting everywhere, trying to take it all in. The sandy shore, the sea gulls and pelicans, the families calling noisily to each other.

And then they saw the sea, magnificent in all its glory. The waves rolled and crashed, flinging salty spray into the air. Brown pelicans dove like kamikaze pilots on a mission, hurtling into the water and bobbing back up again. Cotton-ball clouds gathered on the horizon.

"Wow!" Chris said, "it's so big." He took off down the beach with Gene behind him. Used to narrow streets and crowded neighborhoods, the boys surrendered to the call of open space and soft sand. They flung their arms to the sky and raced from one end of the beach to the other, pointing, laughing, and shouting.

"Look, a seagull," Gene said. "I seen one in a book before, but never for real."

They gathered seashells like jewels, filling their pockets with their sandy treasures. A starfish prompted an up-close examination and a dozen questions. Seals and dolphins frolicked offshore, making the boys laugh with delight. Everywhere they turned, they found something new to marvel at.

I suspect we'll act a lot like Chris and Gene when we get to heaven.

At first we'll stare—overwhelmed by the vast expanse of eternity. Golden streets will glisten in the light of the Son, and family members will call from behind the veil, welcoming us home.

The expanse of eternity will stretch before us, and we'll run with winged feet on golden pavement, shackled no longer to the asphalt of mortality.

Everywhere we turn we'll see gold, jewels, and precious stones. I wonder if we'll stoop to fill our pockets only to realize pockets are no longer needed. The wealth of heaven exists for all. In every direction, we'll find something new to marvel at.

"I read about it in a Book," we'll say, "but I've never seen it for real."

At the center of it all, we'll see God, magnificent in all His glory, seated on His throne while waves of worship crash around Him. Cherubim and seraphim will hover overhead. In the distance, a rainbow cloud will encircle Him.

God will rise from His throne to wash the graffiti of sickness and death off the concrete jungle of our existence. "Behold," He'll say, "I make all things new" (Revelation 21:5 NKJV). He'll restore the world to the beauty it had before sin took a bite out of its perfection.

Exhausted by his adventure, Gene fell asleep on the ride back to the inner city. His mother met them outside their home and carried him in, tucking him gently into bed. She told them later he'd slept straight through until morning. As the sun peeked into his room, his mother heard him rustling. He opened his eyes, rubbed them, and peered at her in sleepy confusion.

"Did I really go there?" he said. "Or was it just a dream?"

On the day we close our eyes on earth and awaken in heaven, we'll wonder the same thing.

Then we'll look into Jesus's eyes, and we'll know.

"Behold," He'll say, as He takes us into His arms. "I make all things **new**."

.

Notes

1. Cathy Lynn Grossman, "Billy Graham's Quotes about Heaven: 'I'm Just Passing through This World,'" *USA Today*, February 21, 2018, https://www.usatoday.com/story/news/nation/2018/02/21/billy-grahams-most-notable-quotes/858852001.

2. Kayla Root, "'Someday You Will Hear Billy Graham Is Dead. Don't Believe a Word of It': His 7 Best Quotes about Heaven," CBN News, February 25, 2018, https://tinyurl.com/m53bcut7.

3. Root, "Someday You Will Hear."

4. Strong's Concordance, s.v. "*hārâ*," BlueLetterBible.org, accessed June 8, 2023, https://www.blueletterbible.org/lexicon/h2734/niv/wlc/0-1.

5. Oswald Chambers, *My Utmost for His Highest* (Grand Rapids, MI: Discovery House, 1963), May 25. First published 1927.

6. "The Westminster Shorter Catechism," APuritansMind.com, accessed June 8, 2023, https://www.apuritansmind.com/westminster-standards/shorter-catechism.

7. Leah MarieAnn Klett, "Chinese Christians Memorize Bible in Prison: Gov't 'Can't Take What's Hidden in Your Heart,'" *Christian Post*, June 11, 2019, https://bit.ly/2XF5McS.

8. Dictionary.com, s.v. "pride," accessed June 8, 2023, https://www.dictionary.com/browse/pride.

9. C. S. Lewis, *The Lion, the Witch and the Wardrobe* (New York: HarperCollins, 1994), 19. First published 1950.

10. "Billy Graham, in Rare Public Appearance, Meets with George W. Bush in North Carolina," Fox News, June 26, 2017, https://www.foxnews.com/politics/billy-graham-in-rare-public -appearance-meets-with-george-w-bush-in-north-carolina.

11. Strong's Concordance, s. v. "*theopneustos*," BlueLetterBible.org, accessed June 8, 2023, https://www.blueletterbible.org/lexicon /g2315/kjv/tr/0-1.

12. Angel E. Navidad, "Marshmallow Test Experiment and Delayed Gratification," Simply Psychology, November 27, 2020, https://www.simplypsychology.org/marshmallow-test.html.

13. If you're looking for a place to start, I recommend the following: www.blueletterbible.org, www.desiringgod.org, *Simply Put* podcast (www.ligonier.org/podcasts/simply-put), Wisdom International wisdomonline.org, www.revive ourhearts.org, and Ligonier Ministries (www.ligonier.org).

About the Author

Lori Hatcher is an author, women's ministry speaker, editor, blogger, career health-care professional, and pastor's wife. A contest-winning Toastmasters International speaker (ACG, ALB), Lori has used stories to impart transformational spiritual truth to women's groups as far away as Mexico and Japan. Lori loves teaching about speaking and nonfiction writing at writers conferences. In fact, Lori loves teaching so much that she homeschooled her daughters from birth to college and lists homeschooling as the hardest and most rewarding accomplishment of her life.

Lori has authored seven devotional books, including *Refresh Your Hope: 60 Devotions for Trusting God with All Your Heart*; *Refresh Your Prayers: Uncommon Devotions to Restore Power and Praise*; *Refresh Your Faith: Uncommon Devotions from Every Book of the Bible*; and the 2016 Christian Small Publisher Book of the Year, *Hungry for God . . . Starving for Time*. She collaborated with her husband, David, to write *Moments with God for Couples*.

Lori also writes devotions for Our Daily Bread Ministries and Guideposts projects including *God Knows Her*, *All God's Creatures*, and *Evenings with Jesus*. Her work has been published by Revive Our Hearts, Proverbs 31 Ministries, *The Upper Room*, *War Cry*, *Today's Christian Living*, and *Christian Living in the Mature Years*.

Lori lives delightfully close to her four grandchildren in Lexington, South Carolina, with her husband and her vast collection of books. Connect with her at www.LoriHatcher.com.

Random Facts about Lori

- She was born in Rhode Island to a Portuguese-Italian mother and a Southern grits–eating father.

- She can sing "Jingle Bells" in Portuguese (the only skill she retained from two years of high school language study).

- She delivered newspapers during the blizzard of '78 and still hasn't thawed out. She shivers if the temperature drops below seventy.

- She chose to study dental hygiene because it required no higher math.

- She hates coffee, loves ice cream, and keeps a stash of miniature Reese's Peanut Butter Cups handy at all times.

- She's read the Bible through approximately twenty times. Her copy of the *John MacArthur Daily Bible* is so worn it sheds fake leather bits every time she opens it. But it's still her favorite.

- She taught Sunday school in a movie theater, delivered a women's ministry presentation in the dark during a tornado warning, and won several Toastmasters International speaking contests.

- She thanks God every day for allowing her to do what she loves—write and speak to encourage others to fall in love with God and His Word.

Spread the Word
by Doing One Thing.

- Give a copy of this book as a gift.

- Write a review of this book on your blog,
  favorite bookseller's website or at
  ourdailybreadpublishing.org.uk

- Recommend this book to your church,
  small group, or book club.

Connect with us. 🄵 🄾 🐦

Our Daily Bread Publishing
PO Box 3566, Grand Rapids, MI 49501, USA
Email: books@odb.org

renew,
refresh,
reclaim

In a world that disappoints again and again, your
heavenly Father does not. Wherever you are
today and whatever your situation tomorrow,
know on a whole new level that God is with you,
He is for you, and He will never fail you.

Well-loved author, blogger, pastor's wife,
and women's ministry speaker Lori Hatcher
is here to help renew, refresh, and reclaim your
confidence in the rock-solid truths about God.

Our Daily Bread
Publishing.